Martine Audéoud

Research as Worship in the Company of God

Christian Scholars Formation Series

Edited by D. Keith Campbell

in cooperation with the Society of Christian Scholars
and the Department of Theological Concerns
of the World Evangelical Alliance

Volume 2

Vol 1   Paul M. Gould et al.: The Outrageous Idea of the Missional Professor (International Edition).
Vol 2   Martine Audéoud: Research as Worship in the Company of God

Martine Audéoud

Research as Worship
in the Company of God

WIPF & STOCK · Eugene, Oregon

Wipf and Stock Publishers
199 W 8th Ave, Suite 3
Eugene, OR 97401

Research as Worship in the Company of God
By Adeoud, Martine
Copyright © 2023 Verlag für Kultur Und Wissenschaft All rights reserved.
Softcover ISBN-13: 978-1-6667-7608-9
Hardcover ISBN-13: 978-1-6667-7609-6
Publication date 3/28/2023
Previously published by Verlag für Kultur Und Wissenschaft, 2023

Contents

Illustrations 7
    Tables..8
    Preface..9

Why Another Research Guide?..13
    What Is the Purpose of This Guide?..13
    Why Use Metaphors to Discuss Research Methods?..................................13
    How Does This Research Guide Connect with Other Research
        Method Books?..14
    Can We Do Research in the Company of God?..14
    May I Thank Several Members of My Company of God?..........................15

Chapter 1: Research as Worship?..17
    Can We Enter into God's Presence?...17
    Can Research Be Integrated in Our Relationship with God?....................18
    How Do Christian Researchers Prepare for Worship?..............................19
    What Are the Three Qualities of Research Developed with God?..........21
        New..21
        Living..21
        Open...22
    An Unpredictable Love-Dance: Nehemiah's Example 22
        An Appreciative Quest 22
        A Relational and Incarnational Quest 23
        A Creative and Life-giving Approach 25
    Next Step...28
    How Can You Creatively Summarize This Chapter?.................................29

Chapter 2: What Is the Problem? 31
    Personal Readiness to Do Research 32
    What Is Your Identity as a Researcher?..34
    What Is Your Problem Statement?..35
    What Is Your Purpose Statement or Research Objective?.....................38
    What Is Your General Research Question?..39
    What Are Your Specific Research Objectives or Questions?.................40
    What Is the Innovative Significance of Your Research?........................42
    What Are the Researcher's Assumptions and Worldviews? 43
    What Are the Delimitations and Limitations of Your Research?.........44

Chapter 3: On What Foundations Will You Build Your Research? 47
What's Next? 45
What Questions Do You Still Have? 46

Chapter 3: On What Foundations Will You Build Your Research? 47
Where Are the Sources of Life? 47
How Is Your Research Guarded? 48
How Shall We Anchor Our Research? 50
What a Colorful Gate! 53
What's Next? 54
Let Us Try to Be Creative! 55

Chapter 4: What Is Your Research Approach? 57
What Research Approaches? 59
What Research Strategies? 61
    Triangulation 61
    Are the Research Instruments Congruent with Research
    Questions? 62
Whom Should Data Be Collected From? (Sampling) 65
How Do Researchers Maintain Integrity in Their Research? 66
What's Next? 69
What Is Your Worshipful Response? 69

Chapter 5: Gathering and Analyzing Data 71
Feeling Overwhelmed? 72
Who Is Our Constant Guide and Safeguard? 73
    How Does the Holy Spirit Support Our Research Work? 73
    How Do We Deal with Our Humanity? 75
    What Is the Role of Prayer in Research? 78
What's Next? 81
Can You Count Your Blessings? 82

Chapter 6: Getting Ready for the Final Offering! 83
What's Next? 90
How Will You Express Your Worship to the Lord? 91

Chapter 7: In God's Presence 93
Going In 94
Going Out 96
A Blessing 97
What about the Humility Gap? 97
What's Next? 98

References 101

Illustrations

Figure 1. *Summary of What Is Needed to Collaborate with God in Research* ... 28
Figure 2. *A fallen tree* ... 37
Figure 3. *Water as One Source of Life* ... 47
Figure 4. *Overview of the Old Testament Tabernacle* ... 48
Figure 5. *Pillars to Anchor Your Research* ... 50
Figure 6. *The Gate of the Tabernacle* ... 53
Figure 7. *The Outer Courtyard* ... 57
Figure 8. *The Bronze Altar* ... 58
Figure 9. *The Research Onion* ... 60
Figure 10. *Data Triangulation* ... 62
Figure 11. *The Bronze Laver* ... 67
Figure 12. *The Holy Place* ... 71
Figure 13. *Overall Picture of the Holy Place* ... 73
Figure 14. *The Golden Candlestick* ... 74
Figure 15. *The Table of the Showbread* ... 76
Figure 16. *The Altar of Incense* ... 78
Figure 17. *Two Views of the Veil of the Holiest Place* ... 83
Figure 18. *The Holiest Place* ... 94

Tables

Table 1. *Research Objectives* 26

Table 2. *Matrix of Main Focus, Objective and Questions* 40

Table 3. *Example of Completed Research Matrix* 41

Table 4. *Example of a Matrix of Main Focus, Questions, and Conceptual or Theoretical Frameworks* 52

Table 5. *The Sacrifices in Leviticus* 58

Table 6 *Research Matrix with Research Instruments* 63

Table 7. *Sample Survey Questions* 64

Table 8. *Dissertation Review Checklist* 85

Preface

This book by Professor Martine Audéoud comes at the right time. When the author contacted me to read her manuscript before writing a preface, I immediately perceived her request as both a privilege and a duty.

It was a privilege because our first contact was only a few years ago, occasioned by the advent of the COVID-19 pandemic. During the lockdown period when universities were almost closed across the continent, I was facilitating video-conference research seminars from March to September 2020, involving postgraduate learners from several countries and universities. In some sessions, many of these African students were recommended by Professor Martine Audéoud. On some other occasions, she also served as a facilitator at our conferences. The same was true for her activities where I was invited to facilitate some modules for both the Christian Alliance University of Abidjan (UACA) and Bakke Graduate University (BGU) where she has academic responsibilities. Since then, our relationship has crystallized around academic issues, especially in the area of scientific research and missiology. It is therefore a privilege to have met her and to preface her book which is of international significance.

Her request also seems to me like a duty, that of understanding the quintessence of her writing before introducing it to the readers. Because this book is a precious treasure that will serve for a long time as a reference tool for doctoral researchers, it becomes imperative to participate in its influence. This duty leads me now to draw readers' attention to the nature, the relevance and the objective as well as the content of this instruction manual.

It is in fact an instruction manual, designed as a learning guide for doctoral students. The author is right: in many places in Africa, for example, where she has served for more than a quarter of a century and continues to serve, many postgraduate students suffer from the lack of a document written in an easily understandable style and related to the methodology of scientific research. However, the unique and somewhat atypical character of this guide lies in the metaphorical approach that also constitutes the nature of the work under review. Designed primarily for a multidisciplinary and Christian student audience, this book uses the metaphor of the biblical tabernacle to show that scientific research is really service to and worship of God. In this sense, the researcher enters the presence of God to discover the hidden things that serve as appropriate solutions to the various problems that this world faces.

It is exactly this aspect that magnifies the relevance of the work in Christian academia. The Christian researcher is thus faced with the duty to participate in the healing and transformation of this world, broken and riddled by questions without appropriate solutions to its contexts. Now, God alone who knows the true needs and the true solutions invites the human being to discover the hidden things still unknown (cf. Jeremiah 33:3). Honest and objective scientific research thus becomes both an academic and spiritual effort to discover unknown, lesser known or poorly known solutions. The tabernacle metaphor of biblical times included the court, the holy place, and the most holy place. If one were to take the same metaphorical approach, one could immediately identify the above-mentioned aspects of discovery, namely the exploration of unknown (most holy place), lesser-known (holy place) or poorly known (court) truths. Scientific research thus becomes a necessity for Christian academics to help the world find more and more appropriate solutions to its innumerable and multifaceted problems. Christian researchers are, therefore, a gift of God to the helpless humanity.

This justifies the objective of this instruction manual, helping to guide Christian researchers toward a profound and integral approach to scientific research. This holistic aspect that Dr. Martine proposes is missing in many books on research methods. It insists on the fact that the problems facing the world require answers that escape human effort alone. In this book, the reader will discover the essential elements of life-giving scientific research.

In addition to the introductory section devoted to the rationale for the book, the document slowly, surely, and methodically unveils the meaning and essence of research as an act of worship. Christian researchers will realize that the approach advocated by this book in its first five chapters is similar to the "problem, literature, methodology, result, and discussion" style, but laid out in a very innovative way, adding an aspect that is lacking in many works aligned with this classic model that has become woefully inadequate in many contexts.

Apart from the metaphorical approach of the work, another innovative aspect is the importance it places on the solution of the real problem to give life. This vitalist approach is to be emphasized! The last two chapters reflect this, speaking respectively of the metaphor of preparation for the final offering and that of the duty to dwell in the presence of God. This is the apotheosis of the innovative contribution of this book, which I would like to see in any library where the promotion of holistic scientific research is on the agenda. As one could say, to a shattered world a holistically appropriate remedy. Dr. Martine Audéoud's book places such a requirement before the researcher.

Dr. Fohle Lygunda li-M, D.Min., Ph.D.
Professor of missiology and researcher in contextual theology
Head of Tearfund's theological department for Africa

Why Another Research Guide?

The need for this guide has been on my heart for many months, if not years. For several years, I have taught and co-taught research methodology classes in Christian institutions. And I have kept asking myself: what are the specificities of teaching and doing research in a Christian institution? As I pondered this question, I became convinced that academic research is *not* disconnected from our Christian faith but should actually be the outcome of our Christian faith. Our faith in Jesus Christ is not a side product of rigorous academic research, but the key focus and raison d'être of our academic research. Since we are *in Christ* (John 15) and since for each of us *to live is Christ* (Phil. 1:21), all that we think, plan, and do should be for His glory (1 Cor. 10:31). Doing doctoral research and writing it up is thus also to be done for God's glory as an act (and a process) of worship.

What Is the Purpose of This Guide?

The purpose of this book is to guide the Christian *doctoral* researcher along a rigorous academic journey with a realization that the outcome of the research, i.e. the doctoral dissertation, is actually the outcome of a faith journey to discover more truth about God, His creation, and the communities of people He left here on earth. This journey stems from God's calling on researchers to accomplish part of their missional calling here on earth. Research entails an effort to learn and understand more truth (all of which originates in God) in order to create more of God's *shalom* here on earth and in the researcher's particular communities. Thus, research is part of the worship offering that Christian researchers are called to bring to God. The outcome of the research journey will culminate in a final act of worship in the presentation of the doctoral dissertation. The term 'doctoral' is not repeated henceforth, but this guide discusses doctoral research specifically, although other kinds of academic research might benefit from this text.

Why Use Metaphors to Discuss Research Methods?

In this book, the metaphors found in the tabernacle, the Jewish worship activities conducted in the desert, and other biblical examples are used to anchor researchers' thoughts and understanding in biblical imagery that might help to illuminate the various stages of the research journey. These metaphors are used to avoid drifting into theoretical or abstract discussions, because in many cultures, ideas may be more strongly anchored by metaphors, images, and pictures.[1] I hope that the references to the Israelites' journey in the desert and their worship practices will help researchers root their work more deeply in their intimacy with God.

How Does This Research Guide Connect with Other Research Method Books?

The Israelites of old were ordered by God to take with them the jewelry and precious wealth of the Egyptians when they left Egypt. These items proved very helpful when the Israelites built the tabernacle and its associated items. Likewise, this guide will refer to research books and materials written by secular writers. God has provided wisdom to all human beings. This wisdom is very obvious in excellent research method books, which were perhaps written under the Holy Spirit's guidance without the writer being aware of it, much as King Cyrus in the Old Testament was accomplishing God's call without being conscious of it.

Can We Do Research in the Company of God?

The other focus of the book's title points to the reality that research is never done alone. Research is done *in the company of God* as an innovation process. It is done in community. Vincent (2016) states:

> The phrase "company of God" reminds us of God's presence, purpose and activity, it also implies the distinct possibility that others God chooses to involve in God's company—other individuals and companies—may not be ones we would choose. It's God's company after all, not ours. (p. 130)[2]

Throughout the phases outlined in this guide, please keep in mind that you are doing your research in the company of God!

---

[1] You may want to read an excellent article from Richardson (2011) on the use of metaphors in cross-cultural communication. Wormelly's (2009) book on using metaphors and analogies in teaching can also be helpful.

[2] You will highly benefit from reading Vincent's (2016) whole book, especially the last chapter. Since research focuses on finding out more about God's truth in the communities we serve, the outcome of research will be enhanced by a deeper understanding of the biblical foundations of innovation as laid out by Vincent. Another helpful text is John Allan Knight's and Ian S. Markham's (2022). It focuses on research in the realm of theology, but it contains some excellent information relevant to Christian researchers in other fields.

May I Thank Several Members of My Company of God?

This guide would never have been completed without a whole team contributing to it! First, I would like to thank all those who have encouraged me throughout the writing process! Many people, at some point, have held me accountable, given me feedback, or provided connections in an exceptionally faithful manner. My special thanks also go to Bakke Graduate University[3] colleagues and students, as they have provided feedback, encouragements, and ideas for improvements. Dr. Judi Melton has been an exceptional support in reviewing and reshaping the document tirelessly. The Society of Christian Scholars, especially Dr. Keith Campbell, and the World Evangelical Alliance, represented by long-time friend Dr. Tom Johnson, have graciously provided an opportunity to publish this document. Dr. Bruce Barron, senior editor for the WEA and the Society of Christian Scholars, has helped to adjust the imperfections that come with English being my third language. I am also very thankful to Dr. Stan Nussbaum, who has very graciously allowed me to capture some practical or pedagogical suggestions from his book, and to Pastor Frederick Travier[4] who allowed me to use the photos of his model of the tabernacle. Finally, last but not least, I am so thankful for my company of prayer partners who have been praying for me and for this project to come to fruition!

May the Triune God be glorified through these reflections and may each of you who are called by God to do specific investigations be encouraged to worship Him through your research!

 Throughout this guide, you will see this sign. It is an idea borrowed from Stan Nussbaum (2007). This sign will invite you to pause, reflect, pray, and possibly take some notes in your personal journal. I highly encourage you to keep a personal journal throughout your research journey.

---

[3] www.bgu.edu
[4] https://frederictravier.fr/le-tabernacle/

Chapter I: Research as Worship?

> Therefore, brothers and sisters, since we have confidence to enter the Most Holy Place by the blood of Jesus, by a new and living way opened for us through the curtain, that is, his body, and since we have a great priest over the house of God, let us draw near to God with a sincere heart and with the full assurance that faith brings, having our hearts sprinkled to cleanse us from a guilty conscience and having our bodies washed with pure water. Let us hold unswervingly to the hope we profess, for he who promised is faithful. And let us consider how we may spur one another on toward love and good deeds, not giving up meeting together, as some are in the habit of doing, but encouraging one another—and all the more as you see the Day approaching. (Heb. 10:19–25, NIV)

You may wonder what this passage from the Bible has to do with research! Actually, each of us, as we enter into God's presence in humility, joy, and awe, is doing research as we seek to understand *who* God is, *why* we are allowed in His presence, and *how* this affects our relationships with the communities we are involved in. Doing research is nothing other than entering into God's presence. Research in academia, which is the focus of this guide, is a smaller part of the larger concept of research. For purposes of simplification, we will understand research in an academic setting as work that is validated within communities of scholars in the scientific world and attempts to solve a given problem or situation.

The joy of doing research to know God will be at the core of our discussions. This guide seeks to strengthen Christian researchers' understanding of the high calling that is placed on their life when they undertake research. Similarly, we will review the challenges of such research as an example of the challenges involved in fully worshipping our God.

Can We Enter into God's Presence?

To frame our reflections on research in reference to the Bible passage quoted above, we must remember that the main problem that we humans have to solve is the problem of sin, which has barred every human being from completely entering into and enjoying God's presence. Through Christ's blood shed on the cross and His victorious resurrection, God has made it possible to enter into His presence freely. Therefore, research is a calling to collaborate with God in His presence to solve problems (created by sin). We can liken this calling to the function of Moses, who led the Hebrews in the desert and entered into God's presence to receive His thoughts and direction so that he could communicate them to the people.

Research represents an attempt to enter into God's presence and understand His truth, His revelation of Himself, His thoughts, His multifaceted perspective on His creation, and His heart for the human beings whom He created. It represents a desire to be more in harmony with Him, to become better co-creators according to His heart. Without delving too far into theological debate, I would suggest that all human beings are called to continue or develop God's initial act of creation and redemption: "We are called to be co-creators with God. Therefore, work must be understood as a participation in the reign of God ... [and] participation in the creative and redemptive work of God" (Harrison, 2004, p. 239).[5] Research is no exception. There is no dichotomy between our work as researchers and 'the rest of our work' that we can do in other aspects of God's calling on our lives. Our ultimate goal as researchers, as well as in other areas of work, is to participate actively in God's ongoing creative and redemptive work, with the ultimate perspective that all our research work will be ultimately brought into subjection to Christ (1 Cor. 15:27–28) so that all may be done to God's glory (1 Cor. 10:31).

Can Research Be Integrated in Our Relationship with God?

Perhaps our African brothers and sisters have a competitive edge, in terms of integrating our research with our spiritual lives, over researchers who grew up in Western cultures. Most of the research frameworks and literature regarding research have been elaborated in Western cultures and have been framed by Greco-Roman philosophies and worldviews. For decades (if not centuries), research methodologies have been dichotomized between quantitative and qualitative approaches, although mixed approaches have been validated in more recent years. The enemy of our souls dichotomizes (i.e. divides in two) and brings death. A very powerful image of this truth is Solomon threatening to divide the only surviving baby and thus kill him (1 Kings 3:16–28).

On the other hand, I invite you to pay attention to non-Western cultures that may often support a much more integrative, holistic and systemic approach to life, and thus also to research more specifically. Having had extensive experience in African cultures, I have observed that African

---

[5] Harrison analyzes how Dorothy Sayers has understood work in terms of demonstrating God's glory through work as we are co-creating with God.

traditional cultures don't view life in categories or boxes. Life is an integrated whole, in which spirituality and spiritual relationships are an integral part of thinking and doing in all spheres of life and in work more specifically. Research can be viewed from this perspective as completely integrated and embedded in our relationship with the Trinity.

At the highest level, God invites the researcher to come to Him, the Triune Creator, and to join His mission (*missio Dei*). Therefore, research and investigation are holy ground and a worship process as the researcher seeks to enter into God's thoughts holistically, to better understand them, in order to collaborate with our Triune God in His creative work both locally and globally. As Lygunda li-M (2018) wrote, "Research projects are not undertaken just to satisfy personal curiosity or for just an academic degree ... [but] in order to address an existential problem which relates to God's glocal and holistic mission" (p. 358). With such a perspective, how does one prepare to enter in God's presence?

How Do Christian Researchers Prepare for Worship?

As Hebrews 10:19–25 stated, the foundation of the Christian researcher's calling is the blood of Christ. Conducting research as a response to God's call on one's life is possible only because Christ's blood has been shed on the cross to give to the researcher full access into God's presence. Therefore, Christ's sacrifice and his resurrection are the foundation of the incredible freedom from which the researcher can now benefit when entering into God's sanctuary and discovering more about God's creative and sustaining power in this world. Thus, *research is worship,* and it is a worship offering as well as a worship process.

When they were offering sacrifices to God, the Jewish priests in the Old Testament went through a very clear process of investigation of the animal to be sacrificed,[6] from the outside examination of its purity and adequacy for the sacrifice through all the steps to prepare for and perform the actual sacrifice. It was a highly regulated process that took time, reflection, assessments, planning, and organizing before one could finally complete the worship process and commune with God and with those bringing or taking part in this offering. This worship process of old can be viewed as an image of the worship process of the researcher.

The Jewish priests of old, before they even proceeded to the point of sacrifice, had to perform some purification duties to be able to offer sacrifices. They had to wash, wear certain clothes, and put themselves person-

---

[6] See for instance the first few chapters of Leviticus.

ally in the condition required by God to offer a sacrifice. Similarly, Christian researchers are called to set their hearts, thoughts, and whole beings in sync with the heart of God. The researcher's personal relationship with God needs to be pure, expressing God's holiness and love. This intimacy with God then leads the researcher to inquire about problems to be solved with and from God's perspective.

Examples from the secular world can show us that holistic approaches to research are not new. The concepts of *appreciative inquiry* as developed by Copperrider and Whitney (2005) or the *constructivist approach* in education promoted by Piaget (1972) may help us gain a better understanding of God's perspective and grasp how to address problematic situations to be reflected on with God. These theoretical frameworks look at situations and people with a definite commitment to discovering the assets, capacities, skills, and resources that one can build on. They are like rays of God's life-giving approaches that have been interpreted and conceptualized in scientific ways. They embody, in their specific ways, powerful instances where researchers, even perhaps without realizing it, sought to come more in tune with God's perspectives on the areas they reflected on, such as business (Cooperrider, 2005) or human development (Piaget, 1972).

Christian researchers are called to prepare their hearts, their minds, and all their lives to be most congruent with the heart of God who seeks to breathe life into everything He does and creates and who calls them to choose life (Deut. 30:19). This approach definitely calls for a reframing of the researcher's life and for ridding oneself of all that can distract from being in God's presence (Matt. 5:28–30). When we are doing research with God, anything that does not align with Him in our lives, habits, and thoughts needs to be taken away so that we can "gain Christ" (Phil. 3:7–11). Research with and for Christ demands that all our focus be in and on Him.

You may want to take time now before the Lord and search your heart. What are the deepest motives of your heart as you anticipate conducting your research? Do you want to get a diploma, or do you really want to partner with God in His mission? Read Psalm 139 and write some of your thoughts and prayers in your notebook.

As a consequence of this yielding, as a researcher, you will discover a *new way* (Heb. 10:19–25) by doing research hand in hand with Him! Let us ponder now this new way that invites us to embark on a journey with God.

Chapter I: Research as Worship?

What Are the Three Qualities of Research Developed with God?

Hebrews 10:20 invites us to enter into a way that is characterized by three qualities: new, living, and open. How does research done in companionship with God demonstrate these three qualities?

New

Developing research is not just describing what exists; it also involves bringing about or proposing new methods, systems, theories, or approaches. We do research because there is a problem that needs to be solved in a *new* way. In the same way as the Christian is called to live in *newness* of life, Christian researchers are called to seek to bring *newness* of life in their research as part of their life-offering to God. What could this newness look like in view of your anticipated research?

 In your personal journal, draw or jot down a picture of the newness that you are thinking of.

Living

The researcher enters into a *living* way! What an amazing reality! All that God invites the researcher to join in with Him is about life! Research needs to be life-giving and to transform old, unhealthy, destructive, and deathly paradigms into new life. As I have often discussed informally with Lygunda li-M (2018), research carried out by Christian researchers should be *vitalistic*[7] or life-giving to have a transformational impact for Christ's kingdom.[8] All of God's work throughout history is about giving life as a response to sin and death that have entered into this world. Consequently, researchers are called to transform the traditional paradigms of research, which often remained theoretical and unused on bookshelves, into newness that is life-giving to communities in need. This is where life-giving action research finds its full meaning.

---

[7] Although it is used with a different meaning in philosophical frameworks, Fohle Lygunda li-M has added a new meaning to the term "vitalistic": life-giving or life-generating.

[8] This topic has often been discussed within a large network of Francophone theologians and missiologists developed by Fohle Lygunda li-M over WhatsApp in response to the COVID-19 pandemic.

Open

The Christian researcher is also called to enter into a way that is *open*. Unlimited creativity is available for experimentation in research, in partnership with our creative God. He *opens* ways where there were no ways. Vincent (2016) states that *in the company of God* "expanded potential is freshly awakened. Some call this hope. Others call it encouragement" (p. 134).

 Read aloud in your own mother tongue this verse: "For I am about to do something new. See, I have already begun! Do you not see it? I will make a pathway through the wilderness. I will create rivers in the dry wasteland" (Is. 43:19). Write down in your personal journal something new that the Lord could do as a consequence of your anticipated research!

So what does research look like within these parameters? Let us look at a concrete biblical example, Nehemiah.

An Unpredictable Love-Dance: Nehemiah's Example

In love, the Trinity reveals itself in the creation, redemption, and recreation of an abundance of life in an unpredictable love-dance.[9] As part of this revelation process, the researcher is invited to enter into the movements of such a divine dance through the following Trinitarian paradigms.

An Appreciative Quest

Holding the Trinity's hand, the researcher will move back and forth, right and left, up and down to make an anticipatory, appreciative inventory of the resources of the situation under scrutiny. Nehemiah is a very appropriate example of this research posture. Immersed in God's word (as seen in his prayer in Nehemiah 1), strengthened by the unexpected favor of the king he was serving (Neh. 2:1-8), and profoundly conscious of God's leading (Neh. 1:8), Nehemiah starts his inquiry (Neh. 2:12-16). He takes time to understand the situation and its assets and liabilities from God's perspective, whereas the inhabitants of Jerusalem had become quite accustomed to a very basic and insecure life in their city and had forgotten the city's high calling. This time of prayerful research represented the foundation of Nehemiah's work later on.

Similarly, Christian researchers are invited to seek God's face and embrace His vision for people in desperate situations who need a special di-

---

[9] See for example Richard Rohr's (2016) book.

vine and life-giving impulse. Nussbaum (2007) provides us with the key to the first step of this approach: "Prayer and research are not substitutes for each other" (p. 14). Time spent in communion with the Holy One will be the best initial and ongoing posture of Christian researchers. It will allow us to refocus and realign research objectives with our life-giving God and transform our vision and assessments.

Instead of only finding out about what was missing, Nehemiah took stock of all the materials available to rebuild the walls of Jerusalem. He evaluated the conditions where the inhabitants were living. He also received God's vision for a reconstructed city. He did this part prayerfully, alone, and in silence. In the researcher's life, there are many moments of silence, especially at the beginning, when one does not know how or where to start. Embarking on an unpredictable research journey may involve many such moments of silence and solitude. However, out of these solitary times of tranquil assessment emerged an unprecedented vision. Nehemiah embraced the life-giving challenge of becoming re-creator of the city of Jerusalem in collaboration with his God. He now saw the prevailing situation and its assets and embraced God's love for Jerusalem as he danced with God and rejoiced with Him in anticipation of the final vision of a recreated city. As a consequence, he was ready for the next step.

 As you prayerfully "walk around your city," what are the assets and resources that the Lord is reminding you of? List them in your research journal. Ponder this prayer in Psalm 65:1-4 (NIV):

¹ Praise awaits you, our God, in Zion;
  to you our vows will be fulfilled.
² You who answer prayer,
  to you all people will come.
³ When we were overwhelmed by sins,
  you forgave our transgressions.
⁴ Blessed are those you choose
  and bring near to live in your courts!
We are filled with the good things of your house,
  of your holy temple.

A Relational and Incarnational Quest

Although he held a very high position in the King's entourage, Nehemiah was not lured by its pleasant appeals. Rather, his life was anchored in his Jewish identity and in God's word (at that time, it was the word of the prophets such as Jeremiah). Because of his commitment to loving God and

His people first and foremost, Nehemiah was ready to give up his position and travel to the abandoned city of Jerusalem to live there with God's people. In Jerusalem, he developed relationships and credibility while mobilizing them to change their condition (Neh. 2:17–19). He loved God, he loved His people, and he loved His city.

To move to Jerusalem, Nehemiah had to be clear about who he was and about his identity as a Jewish immigrant in Nebuchadnezzar's kingdom. He had to understand his own worldview and to assess his people's worldview. He had to be extremely clear about his non-negotiable personal values and life commitments as he assessed all aspects of the construction work, including dealing with power sharing and opposition. This clarity of identity can also be noted in the first verses of John 13, where the verb *knowing* is repeated twice, in verses 1 and 3, with very deep descriptions of Jesus' personal assurance about his identity. Obviously Jesus had revealed this identity to his disciples, since John had a very specific understanding of it and could record it in writing. If Christian researchers are not aware of who they are before and in Christ (e.g. John 15), and if they are not clear about their cultural identity and their God-given calling, it will be difficult for them to understand the perceived identity of the communities they serve. Therefore, I often strongly encourage scholars engaging in transformational research to reflect on who they are as Christian scholars and about their calling to scholarship.[10]

Nehemiah's holistic and incarnational approach to his work is noteworthy. He walks and talks with his people, researches his city in its darkest times, develops relationships with the leaders of his people and feeds them, and undoubtedly much more! He looks at his mission from all angles. I am reminded of our dear brother René Padilla, world-renowned theologian and missiologist who went to be with the Lord in 2022. He was the herald of a holistic approach to mission from the time of his powerful Lausanne address in 1974 up through the Cape Town Commitment in 2010, where the holistic shape of missions was completely integrated. Why speak about holistic mission here? Because research should be done not just for the sake of developing theory, but to bring transformational life to communities affected by the research. Developing such research quests will be part of a holistic perspective on missions; that is, a Christian researcher will complete research to contribute to the Church's missional calling on earth. Therefore, a loving, incarnational, and holistic approach to communities under study is non-negotiable for creative and life-giving research to take place.

---

[10] The Society of Christian Scholars can provide very helpful resources in this reflection. See https://scshub.net/.

A Creative and Life-giving Approach

As co-creators with God, we are called, in our finitude, to develop a research project that reflects who He is: a creative, redemptive, and life-giving God. God has called us to "reign in life through the one man, Jesus Christ" (Rom. 5:17). Thus, research cannot be dissociated from the fullness of life that Christ has provided to us through His blood shed on the cross and his victory over death. The understanding and experience of the power of Christ's life throughout the research process are fully embedded in two aspects of God's gift to each believer (Rom. 5:17):

- God's *abundant* provision of **grace** and
- God's *gift* of **righteousness**.

Christian researchers, to develop life-giving research, should be rooted and immersed in the lavishness of God's grace and the freedom of God's righteousness. God's overflowing and manifold (1 Peter 4:10) grace will sustain us throughout our research, and it will also allow us to enter into God's creative thinking to hand out and give away His grace through new and life-giving perspectives, processes, proposals, findings, and recommendations. Thus, we will experience God's creative joy and overflowing grace as described in Isaiah 43:17:

> See, I am doing a new thing!
>   Now it springs up; do you not perceive it?
> I am making a way in the wilderness
>   and streams in the wasteland.

The abundance of God's grace that will unfold through our research will be deployed hand in hand with the free gift (sorry about the pleonasm, but this redundancy originated with Paul!) of His *righteousness.* God's righteousness has been fully satisfied at the cross by Christ's death and resurrection. We understand this often in relationship only to our sins, or sometimes we expand the concept to distressing situations in our communities. However, a wider understanding of God's righteousness in all arenas of our lives, including academic and community-transforming research, will provide a solid foundation of the *ethical aspects* of our research. Because of God's righteousness that has been imparted to us, we must embed our research processes within His righteousness—which means, in less theological terms, within ethical and moral paradigms, processes, and frameworks that are fully congruent with His righteousness. Because of the cross and the resurrection, Christian researchers will seek to demonstrate to their utmost understanding God's life-giving *shalom*, which is embedded in His overflowing grace and deepest righteousness.

Coming back to our biblical researcher Nehemiah, we see throughout his book how he implemented his research findings while embedding them in God's grace and righteousness. Nehemiah organized the building of the walls with order and avoided any compromise with his enemies or with people who were not single-minded for God (see for example Nehemiah 4 and 5). Meanwhile, he provided abundant food for his people (Neh. 5:14-19), thus demonstrating God's abundant grace. As a consequence, fullness of joy was experienced when they assessed the outcomes (Neh. 12:24, 27, 43), and the promise of Nehemiah 8:10 came to complete fruition: "The joy of the Lord is your strength." We can also surely assume that the monuments constructed, i.e. the walls and houses surrounding the city, were creatively sculpted and artistically decorated. God's creativity was demonstrated through the builders' creativity, bringing joy to the whole city. This is also what should happen when the outcomes of our research are shared and implemented. God's creative beauty will be witnessed by and will bring joy to the stakeholders or beneficiaries of our research as well as the research community.

From a practical perspective, for Christian researchers embarking on a research project, I would like to share the following research objectives as guidelines and checkpoints. These objectives have been adapted from BGU's Ph.D. program outcomes (Table 1).

Table 1: Research Objectives

Criteria	Researcher's Objectives
Spiritual Formation – How will this research help you, as a Christian Researcher, to have increased trust in God while dynamically developing and stewarding your partnerships and networks?	• Demonstrate a biblical or theological basis for innovation in your life and research work, especially in the context of authentic community. • Demonstrate personal spiritual growth that significantly demonstrates righteous and graceful relationships with God, self, others, and creation.
Perspective – What shifts in worldview, mindset, new ways of	• Engage in and facilitate research in innovation and trans-

Chapter I: Research as Worship? 27

seeing yourself, God, and others will result from this research?

Knowledge – What knowledge is needed to accomplish spiritual formation and perspective transformation?

Skills – What hands-on skills have you learned, demonstrated, and evaluated throughout your research?

Application – How will you apply the outcome of your research in your life and work?

formation to harness a culture of innovation and creativity.

- Facilitate innovative community transformation in while embracing the following eight perspectives of transformational leadership to advance God's kingdom: calling-based, incarnational, reflective, servant, contextual, *shalom*, prophetic, and global.

- Demonstrate that you have acquired knowledge and understanding of how to conduct and apply research innovatively to the challenges and assets of the communities served.

- Demonstrate the ability to conduct innovative, quality research, including a wide variety of research methodologies, combined with excellent communication.

- Demonstrate the ability to lead organization, community and team innovation while using (a) proficiency in theories of organization and team innovation, and (b) knowledge of how leadership styles and community culture impact community innovation.

- Use and apply measures of innovation in a significant transformation while

- identifying contextualized best practices of innovative leadership;

- articulating why leaders need innovation;
- identifying knowledge of the value of an innovative transformational model to a community; and
- helping community leaders identify their community's innovative profile.

Next Step

Throughout this chapter, we have walked on holy ground while realizing the privilege of entering into God's holy and loving presence to do collaborative and creative research with him. It is such a privilege to embrace our role as co-creators with Him! Figure 1 summarizes very briefly what this involves on the researcher's side.

Figure 1: Summary of What Is Needed to Collaborate with God in Research

The next chapter will introduce the various elements needed to frame God-centered, community-focused, worshipful research. There we will use many elements of the Jewish worship processes in the tabernacle as metaphors.

How Can You Creatively Summarize This Chapter?

I highly encourage you, after you have reflected on this chapter, to write a poem, create or record a song, make an illustration, or use some other creative way to communicate to God and commune with Him regarding your heart's desire for your research.

Chapter 2: What Is the Problem?

The Day of Atonement
(Leviticus 16 – NIV)

The LORD spoke to Moses after the death of the two sons of Aaron who died when they approached the LORD. The LORD said to Moses: "Tell your brother Aaron that he is not to come whenever he chooses into the Most Holy Place behind the curtain in front of the atonement cover on the ark, or else he will die. For I will appear in the cloud over the atonement cover.

"This is how Aaron is to enter the Most Holy Place: He must first bring a young bull for a sin offering and a ram for a burnt offering. He is to put on the sacred linen tunic, with linen undergarments next to his body; he is to tie the linen sash around him and put on the linen turban. These are sacred garments; so he must bathe himself with water before he puts them on. From the Israelite community he is to take two male goats for a sin offering and a ram for a burnt offering.

"Aaron is to offer the bull for his own sin offering to make atonement for himself and his household. Then he is to take the two goats and present them before the LORD at the entrance to the tent of meeting. He is to cast lots for the two goats—one lot for the LORD and the other for the scapegoat. Aaron shall bring the goat whose lot falls to the LORD and sacrifice it for a sin offering. But the goat chosen by lot as the scapegoat shall be presented alive before the LORD to be used for making atonement by sending it into the wilderness as a scapegoat.

"Aaron shall bring the bull for his own sin offering to make atonement for himself and his household, and he is to slaughter the bull for his own sin offering. He is to take a censer full of burning coals from the altar before the LORD and two handfuls of finely ground fragrant incense and take them behind the curtain. He is to put the incense on the fire before the LORD, and the smoke of the incense will conceal the atonement cover above the tablets of the covenant law, so that he will not die. He is to take some of the bull's blood and with his finger sprinkle it on the front of the atonement cover; then he shall sprinkle some of it with his finger seven times before the atonement cover.

"He shall then slaughter the goat for the sin offering for the people and take its blood behind the curtain and do with it as he did with the bull's blood: He shall sprinkle it on the atonement cover and in front of it. In this way he will make atonement for the Most Holy Place because of the uncleanness and rebellion of the Israelites, whatever their sins have been. He is to do the same for the tent of meeting, which is among them in the midst of their uncleanness. No one is to be in the tent of meeting from the time Aaron goes in to make atonement in the Most Holy Place until he comes out, having made atonement for himself, his household and the whole community of Israel.

"Then he shall come out to the altar that is before the LORD and make atonement for it. He shall take some of the bull's blood and some of the goat's blood and put it on all the horns of the altar. He shall sprinkle some of the blood on it with his finger seven times to cleanse it and to consecrate it from the uncleanness of the Israelites.

"When Aaron has finished making atonement for the Most Holy Place, the tent of meeting and the altar, he shall bring forward the live goat. He is to lay both hands on the head of the live goat and confess over it all the wickedness and rebellion of the Israelites—all their sins—and put them on the goat's head. He shall send the goat away into the wilderness in the care of someone appointed for the task. The goat will carry on itself all their sins to a remote place; and the man shall release it in the wilderness.

"Then Aaron is to go into the tent of meeting and take off the linen garments he put on before he entered the Most Holy Place, and he is to leave them there. He shall bathe himself with water in the sanctuary area and put on his regular garments. Then he shall come out and sacrifice the burnt offering for himself and the burnt offering for the people, to make atonement for himself and for the people. He shall also burn the fat of the sin offering on the altar."

Personal Readiness to Do Research

You may wonder what this biblical passage has to do with our desire to do research as an expression of our worship of God! Actually, our research seeks to fill a gap or solve a problem that we have identified as crucial to develop God's *shalom* in the communities we serve. This gap or problem has developed as a consequence of sin, which is prevalent in this world.

As you read the Leviticus 16 passage quoted above, you can observe that atonement must be made for Aaron and his household first, and then for the Israelites. Aaron himself had to be purified and to wear clean white linen clothes, which can represent Christ's perfection in His humanity. As a spokesperson for the Israelites before God, Aaron had to offer a bull as a sacrifice for his own sins and those of his household (Lev. 16:11-14). He could not solve the problem of the Israelites' sin without first dealing with his and his household's sin. This example teaches us that if we wish to help in bringing God's solutions to the problems we have identified, we need first to come before God and claim Christ's sacrifice as a redemption for us individually and for our household (or family).

Note that the priest's family is directly included in the purification ritual. Similarly, I would suggest that the "cleanliness" of our family, i.e. our household, be included as much as possible in our prayers for cleanliness, or our sanctification process, before our God. Our lives as researchers, as well as those of our families, must be fully covered by the blood of Christ, represented in Leviticus 16 by the offering of the bull. This is also a reason why I highly encourage researchers to create a *personal learning community* of friends and colleagues who will not only support them in their research and learning, but who will also intercede for their families, bringing them before God in prayer.

Seek the Lord and write in your personal journal a list of three to five accountability partners who can commit to praying for you daily as you develop your research, as well as giving you advice as you move forward in your research. "Victory is won through many advisers" (Prov. 11:14, NIV).

The second section in this chapter (Lev. 16:15ff.) deals with the atonement made for the sins of the Israelites. We don't know what their specific sins were, but we can imagine that there were a multitude of them, from personal sins (like those of Aaron's sons who didn't worship God in the prescribed way in Leviticus 10) to sins performed within their communities (which we can easily imagine) and even in the management of their environment (we see that some animals should not be eaten, for instance). Aaron was the main person managing this atonement. He can also symbolize the role of researchers who, while learning to understand their communities' processes and relationships, have developed a clearer understanding of the gaps where God's *shalom* needs to be promoted or restored. They will thus seek to lead their communities toward developing restored relationships with God, among themselves and with their environment. This atonement was done by the High Priest yearly for the benefit of the whole Israelite community. It behooves us, as researchers, to understand that we function in the role of a high priest before God on behalf of the communities we serve. What a high and extraordinary calling! We are called to walk in the steps of Christ who is our ultimate High Priest (Heb. 4:14; 5:1–10; 6:20; 7:25–28; 8:1–6; 9:11–14). What a sacred calling!

Take time to seek God's face so that you may receive from Him a clearer understanding of the areas where He calls you to live out more of His shalom. Write your thoughts and prayers in your personal research journal.

Two goats had to be specifically chosen. The people's sins were confessed by Aaron at length while he laid his hands on one goat, which had to be sent out into a desert valley. The other goat had to be slaughtered as a sacrifice for God—an image of God's provision in Christ's death to cover the sins of the people.

I would propose that the confession of sins on the *Azazel* or *scapegoat* (Lev. 16:8) can be seen as a metaphor for all the questions researchers will need to ask regarding the main research problem or focus they have identified. Unless relevant and appropriate questions are asked that will guide the investigation of the problem, relevant solutions will not be found. Aaron was very much aware of the people's sins that he had to confess, because he had been living in the midst of his people for a whole year. Similarly, researchers will need to take a very incarnational stance toward the problems for which they seek redemption (the best solution). Incarnational leadership was exhibited by Aaron and also by our High Priest, our Lord Jesus Christ (Phil. 2:6–8; John 1:14–18). Incarnational research will lead us to cultivate trust within the communities where we conduct research, through the development of credible and hopefully very genuine relationships. These relationships will enable researchers to identify what I call *shalom-gaps* in the workings of the community under study and to bring them before God to discern what solutions need to be worked out within the community to increase and expand the *shalom* there.

Reflect on the communities that your research will affect. What are they? What are their worldviews, their history, and their specificities? Bring them prayerfully to the Lord. Then write in your research journal a thorough description of the context of the communities you will serve through your research. This could then be reviewed and integrated into the context section of the first chapter of your proposal.

What Is Your Identity as a Researcher?

As we consider the imagery of the Tabernacle and the Hebrews' worship in the desert, I invite you to focus on how the High Priest was clothed

(Exod. 28). He had such beautiful clothes, and interesting interpretations of the meaning of the different parts of his garments can be found. You may want to research this topic.[11] Extremely *innovative* skills were required to put these garments together. These garments portrayed extensively who this High Priest was and what his role and purpose in life were in this Jewish context.

The Hebrew High Priest is an image of our Lord Jesus Christ. Hebrews 4:14–16 tells us that Jesus is our High Priest because of his qualifications! He enters for us before God the Father because of his perfection. John 13:1–3, on the other hand, shows us how Christ is perfectly conscious of his *identity* as he serves us (look at the repetition of the verb *knew*). He could not live, act, or interact with his disciples and the communities around him without having had a perfect understanding of his own identity.

Similarly, as researchers seek to follow Christ, the High Priest, in their work, they must identify and discuss what characterizes their identity as well as how these elements can impact the research. So many elements of one's culture, context, or values can affect the scope of and approach to research while possibly also fostering limitations or biases in the research approaches and questions, as well as in the organization of the data gathered, the discussion of these data, and the conclusions and solutions to the problem that will be offered.

Prayerfully, write in your personal research journal a description of who you are and what characterizes your identity that could affect how you conduct your research. This material will then be integrated into a section in your first chapter where you will assess your own assumptions, worldviews, and biases. Pray with David in Psalm 139 (NIV):

²³ Search me, God, and know my heart;
test me and know my anxious thoughts.
²⁴ See if there is any offensive way in me,
and lead me in the way everlasting.

What Is Your Problem Statement?

The biblical text studied in this section focuses on the *main problem*, which is the *sins* the Israelites were committing that prevented them from entering into God's presence and enjoying fellowship with Him. Sin had entered into the world and was also inhabiting the people of Israel, constituting a constant hindrance that prevented a fluid relationship with God. This is

---

[11] The following video can be helpful: https://youtu.be/T6h2KhLtFAg.

what the so-called *Yom Kippur* ceremony was designed to deal with. The sins were identified (spoken out) and sent out on the scapegoat, and the solution to these sins was brought before God with the goat offered as a burnt offering before God in the tabernacle.

Sin is indeed the main source of all the specific problems we identify here on earth, and more precisely the source of the problems that researchers seek to solve through their research. Researchers need to *specifically identify the main problem* they want to concentrate on. Christian researchers are called to identify that main problem *while centering on God's perspective* on that problem in an incarnational way, much as the High Priest lived incarnationally with his people and listened to their pleas. The sacrifice brought by the High Priest represents Christ offering himself as an atonement for sin. It was the basis for a restored life and *shalom* between God and His people. I would propose that Christ's sacrifice and resurrection represent the foundation of the solutions that researchers can look for so as to bring God's *shalom* to problems that have been identified. Christ is our peace (Eph. 4:14). Research with God is rooted in this understanding and realization.

From a *practical research perspective*, the following items must be addressed to answer the question "What is the problem?"—i.e. to identify the *problem statement*.

1. The *problem itself*, i.e. what is going wrong, needs to be clearly identified, stated, and expressed in writing. Here are three examples: (a) "Christian parents are discouraged because their children are leaving the Christian faith." (b) "After 100 Christian disciples were trained over a period of five years in this organization, only five have emerged as spiritual leaders capable of training new disciples." (c) "Since the beginning of the COVID-19 pandemic, our denomination has lost at least 30% of its membership."

2. The *reasons why the problem exists* need to be clarified. In example (a), parents are expecting their children to embrace their own faith in Christ. Example (b) is a problem because of the desire to multiply the number of spiritual leaders through a discipleship effort. In example (c), the growth expectation of a church underlies the problem identification.

3. The *significance* of the problem also needs to be emphasized. In example (a), since faith is at the core of the family's education of their children, the lack of faith creates a huge void in communication and a major culture change in families. Example (b) highlights a major investment in discipleship training and the lack of related outcomes. Example (c) charts a path to imminent church closure, which is contrary to the vision of most churches.

Chapter 2: What Is the Problem? 37

4. You need to clarify the *evidence* that shows that the problem actually exists and is real. In all three examples above, the researchers would need not only to provide statistical data, but also to reflect on the various ways in which the problem is palpable. Researchers also need to elucidate the scope of the problem, the geographical location, the cultural contexts that support expectations, and so on.

5. Finally, at this stage, researchers will need to share *what has already been researched* on the problem that has been researched on. This is where the researcher's knowledge and understanding of the resources of the context under study will be crucial.

Figure 2: A fallen tree

Source: Unknown

Figure 2 can be used to illustrate what we have just discussed. The *problem* is that the car cannot move forward. The *reason* for the problem is the fallen tree blocking the road. The picture provides one piece of *evidence* that the car cannot move. Another piece of evidence is that the car's speedometer reading is zero miles per hour. The *significance* of this research will be supported by the long queue of cars lining up behind the first car in the next few minutes or turning around because the road is blocked or by the availability of a detour. Furthermore, a researcher will need the to find out what prior *research* says, such as regarding the possibility of trees falling on roads if they are planted too close to the side of the road.

Take time to seek the Lord and bring him what you have understood so far as to the problem He wants you to research. In your personal research journal, answer these questions:
- *What is the problem?*
- *Why is it a problem?*
- *What is the significance of this problem?*
- *What is the evidence that shows there is a problem?*
- *What research has already been done regarding this problem or a similar one?*

*As you reflect on this problem, be encouraged by this promise of Deuteronomy 31:6 (NIV): "Be strong and courageous. Do not be afraid or terrified because of them, for the L*ORD *your God goes with you; he will never leave you nor forsake you."*

These five steps will allow you to come up with a crucial element of your research journey: a *purpose statement.*

What Is Your Purpose Statement or Research Objective?

Once you have completed the previous reflection, you will come up with a *purpose statement* that will sum up and clarify the goals and objectives of the proposed study. Creswell (2018) describes what purpose statements need to look like. For the sake of simplicity, here is a purpose statement template: "I anticipate studying ... in order to discover ... so that ... ." Creswell gives excellent examples of such statements. These statements are generally present in the first chapter of doctoral dissertations. For example in Geib's (2020) dissertation research, one can find the purpose of each of the parts of the research in the introductory sections of each chapter, where the overarching purpose is to examine the toxicity of certain drug components, in particular those used in pain alleviation.

Just as the High Priest declared verbally and audibly the sins (problems) that needed to be solved, your purpose statement should clearly and concisely identify the meaning, depth, scope and goals of the intended research. It will constitute the general research objective for your study. In the example of the fallen tree, a purpose statement might be as follows: "I intend to study how one can clear an obstructed road so as to discover the most efficient strategy to enable cars to move forward on this road."

Prayerfully, in less than 20 words, write in your research journal your purpose statement. Include these elements: "I intend to study ... in order to discover... because I want to ..."

What Is Your General Research Question?

You will then turn your purpose statement or general research objective into a general research question that will guide your whole dissertation research. This general research question should flow out of and should be extremely congruent and aligned with your purpose statement. Continuing with our car example, the general research question could be "What is the most efficient way to clear that road so that cars can drive on it?"

This may seem simple, but it will require clear wording that emphasizes your ultimate research objective. Keep in mind that your ultimate goal is to promote God's kingdom *shalom*. As a co-creator with God, you will develop your research with God. While remaining aware of your identity in Christ, you will seek, in your purpose statement and research question, to reflect that your deepest desire is to contribute to extending God's *shalom* in the context and situation you are facing. The deepest goal of your research question will thus contribute to God's overall purpose here on earth, shining forth God's glory through the expansion of His *shalom* in the specific context and situation where He has called you to work.

Read Psalm 10 (NIV) below, and then write a concise main research question in your research journal (don't imitate David in what you write, but in your prayers!).

> ¹ *Why, LORD, do you stand far off?*
> *Why do you hide yourself in times of trouble?*
> ² *In his arrogance the wicked man hunts down the weak,*
> *who are caught in the schemes he devises.*
> ³ *He boasts about the cravings of his heart;*
> *he blesses the greedy and reviles the LORD. ...*
> ¹² *Arise, LORD! Lift up your hand, O God.*
> *Do not forget the helpless.*
> ¹³ *Why does the wicked man revile God?*
> *Why does he say to himself,*
> *"He won't call me to account"?*
> ¹⁴ *But you, God, see the trouble of the afflicted;*
> *you consider their grief and take it in hand.*
> *The victims commit themselves to you;*
> *you are the helper of the fatherless. ...*
> ¹⁷ *You, LORD, hear the desire of the afflicted;*

> you encourage them, and you listen to their cry,
> [18] defending the fatherless and the oppressed,
> so that mere earthly mortals
> will never again strike terror.

What Are Your Specific Research Objectives or Questions?

As you pursue more detailed analysis of what your research questions entail, you will develop more specific questions that will help you develop the various steps in your research. A biblical example of how to develop these specific research questions is the story of Jesus and the Samaritan woman at the well in John 4:1–26. In this encounter, Jesus starts by probing the obvious: He asks for a drink. He seeks to analyze the situation he encounters: is there enough water for him to drink? Second, he probes for deeper understanding of where this woman is spiritually. Does she know God's gift of living waters? Third, he gets to the root of the problem. He asks the woman to get her husband, which leads her to acknowledge her own critical problem and her need for the Messiah. And finally, he leads her to seek the solution she is actually and unknowingly looking for—the Messiah.

Researchers, especially in the social sciences, can use a similar approach when asking their more specific research questions. First, there is a need to *assess* the problematic situation. What are the obvious symptoms that reveal a problem? Such questions often start with WHAT. Second, researchers will look for deeper causes of the obvious problem. They will seek to *go to the root* of the problem and ask WHY questions. Third, they will seek answers or solutions to the problem. These questions could start with WHAT IF.

Table 2 is a matrix that can help you at this stage.

Table 2: Matrix of Main Focus, Objective and Questions

RESEARCH FOCUS	OBJECTIVE	QUESTION
Overall focus		
1st secondary		
2nd secondary		
3rd secondary		
4th secondary		

Using the example of John 4, Table 3 suggests how this research matrix could be filled.

Table 3: Example of Completed Research Matrix

RESEARCH FOCUS	OBJECTIVE	QUESTION
Overall focus	*Seek transformation and freedom for this woman*	*How can this woman be freed from her sinful life?*
1st secondary	*__Describe__ present disruptive water situation*	*How does Jesus' encounter with the woman happen?*
2nd secondary	*Find the __causes__ of her behavior*	*Why does this woman get water in the heat of the day?*
3rd secondary	*Find the __consequences__ of these behaviors*	*What are the consequences of this woman's marital situation?*
4th secondary	*Propose __solutions__ to free this woman to live an integrated community life*	*In what ways will knowing the Messiah transform and free this woman?*

Prayerfully, fill your own research matrix with your research objectives and questions (primary and secondary). Review your research matrix with your personal learning community and possibly with your research supervisor. Pray together over it. Make any changes that you, as a research team, deem necessary. Read Proverbs 2:6-8 (NIV):

[6] For the L<small>ORD</small> gives wisdom;
from his mouth come knowledge and understanding.
[7] He holds success in store for the upright,
he is a shield to those whose walk is blameless,
[8] for he guards the course of the just
and protects the way of his faithful ones.

It is absolutely critical for you to take the time to fill this table adequately. This matrix will constitute the backbone of your overall research and more specifically of the literature review, the research methodology and the strategies adopted, as well as the discussion of the research findings.

What Is the Innovative Significance of Your Research?

Academic researchers must demonstrate to their audience the innovative and transformational significance of their research. Once the research questions have been clearly identified, Christian researchers will be ready to discuss how their work innovatively improves people's lives, communities, organization, or culture in congruence with their deepest desire to develop God's *shalom* in their sphere of influence. Research is not conducted purely for the sake of research. It aims at proposing solutions and improving problematic situations that have resulted from sin. In the footsteps of our High Priest, researchers will reflect on how their research will affect their community. Along the way, it would also be advisable for researchers to analyze the congruence of their research with the core values of the school or program.

For instance, at Bakke Graduate University (2022), researchers must demonstrate how the eight perspectives of transformational leadership that are at the core of each course taught at BGU are embedded in their research:

1. **Calling-Based Leadership.** The leader seeks to understand God-given gifts, experiences, and opportunities so as to understand his or her unique role as a called instrument of Christ's transforming work in and above world cultures.

2. **Incarnational Leadership.** The leader pursues shared experiences, shared plights, shared hopes, and shared knowledge and tasks.

3. **Reflective Leadership.** The leader lives in reality, reflects on its meaning, and catalyzes others with the courage, symbols, and example needed to make meaning in their own lives.

4. **Servant Leadership.** The leader's behavior and priority are on servanthood first. In the style of Jesus, the leader leads by serving and serves by leading.

5. **Contextual Leadership.** The leader recognizes the previous work of God in other cultures and seeks to experience its unique gospel expression.

6. **Global Leadership.** The leader understands the complexity of today's global, pluralistic, urban, economic, and political landscape and sees the Church from the perspective of a world church rather than a nationalized, denominational, or localized church.

7. **Shalom Leadership.** The leader pursues reconciling relationships between people and each other, God, and their environment, as well as with themselves. The leader works toward the well-being, abundance, and wholeness of the community and its member individuals.

8. **Prophetic Leadership.** The leader speaks truth with love to and through power. With sacrifice and humility, the leader pursues change in the broken systems and practices in the political, economic, social, and religious life of the city and world. The leader must give voice to those who have no voice (Prov. 31:8).

Reflect on the core values of your university program. May I suggest that you add a column on the right of your research matrix with the heading "Core Values" and then fill that column for each line? Is there an additional non-negotiable value that the Lord is bringing to your mind and that will be foundational to your research? Include it in your research matrix. Ask the Lord to strengthen you to be faithful to these values, remembering 2 Tim. 2:15 (NIV): "Do your best to present yourself to God as one approved, a worker who does not need to be ashamed and who correctly handles the word of truth."

What Are the Researcher's Assumptions and Worldviews?

We have already seen the need for Christian researchers to become aware of and discuss their own identity as Christian researchers, in the same way as Jesus the High Priest was fully aware of His role and calling among His people. Jesus Christ provides us with examples of assumptions with which He dealt. In John 4, discussed above, He is very aware of the woman's status as an outcast and her assumption that he would not even relate to her in a dialogue, let alone ask for her help. He overcomes the contextual assumptions of the surrounding culture and builds bridges at a higher level.

Another interesting example from Jesus' life is the story of the Syrophoenician woman in Mark 7:24–30. Both Christ and the woman were very conscious of the cultural assumptions surrounding them. The woman jumps ahead and moves the conversation, but also her assumptions, to a higher level—a step that is admired by our Lord.

We could give many other examples from Christ's life where He and the people with whom He interacts deal with their assumptions and worldviews. People often considered their worldviews not as non-negotiable frameworks, but as springboards to move relationships to higher levels. Similarly, understanding one's assumptions as researchers is part of the requisite self-awareness that will allow interactions with the communities being researched to move to a higher (or deeper) level than what was commonly accepted. Again, unless we understand who we are and what assumptions our worldviews carry with them, it will be difficult to challenge them and hopefully advance to other creative possibilities.

Understanding one's cultural frameworks and worldviews (and the assumptions derived from these frameworks) is part of understanding one's identity as a researcher, as stated above. Although describing and analyzing one's worldview would be a good piece of research in itself, researchers are highly encouraged to identify the elements of their worldviews that will affect their research. Becoming increasingly aware of the specific aspects of their worldviews that relate to their creative research will pave the way for researchers entering into God's presence to co-create with Him through research. And when one becomes more aware of one's finitude and the need for a larger or wider framework than one's own, this will hopefully provoke *humility* and the desire to listen and learn more about the truth as the Lord unfolds or unlocks it. This attitude of humility will also produce a great amount of respect toward the community members we seek to research, and it will translate into the opposite of a "savior mentality" that we can sometimes witness in dissertations.

Job is a great example of someone who attempted to research God until God revealed to him how his worldview was so much smaller than God's. This revelation turned his worldview upside down. Perhaps we should seek God's face diligently so that He can reveal Himself to us in a very special and focused way that will enlarge our view of who He is, especially in the context of our research. Our worldview must be heavily influenced by who He is! This will also give us wisdom and humility as we proceed through the details of building the research frameworks and will make us more aware of our biases as researchers so that we can develop a research framework that is more inclusive of God's truth.

Reflect prayerfully on the assumptions and worldviews you bring into your research and how they may affect your research. Write your thoughts in your personal research journal. Write a prayer that expresses your need for wisdom and humility as you proceed through your research.

What Are the Delimitations and Limitations of Your Research?

As a consequence of searching their hearts and minds before the Lord, as noted above, Christian researchers will become much more aware of the delimitations and limitations of their research. Why? Because we are finite human beings. In Genesis 2:8–17, for instance, God gave Adam and Eve a specific scope for the discovery (i.e. research) of the universe in which humans were placed. There was a specific garden (delimitations) and also a limit on what they could access (limitation): the tree of the knowledge of good and evil was not to be touched. God encouraged Adam and Eve to research and enjoy His company as they worshipped Him in the garden. However, overstepping the boundaries set by God will lead to catastrophe, as described in Genesis 3.

Likewise, Christians who develop their research as an act of worshipping God must become very aware of the delimitations, i.e. the scope, of the research to which they are called. Personal understanding and acceptance of the delimitations of one's research calls for an attitude of humility and dependence on God, the Creator and the Redeemer of the specific community or problem that needs redemption. Delimiting the scope of research is an important step as you map out your worshipful calling.

A limitation was given to Adam and Eve as they "researched" their garden in the company of their Creator: submission to God also entailed submission to His order not to touch one element of this garden. Likewise, each research project has limitations that the researcher needs to recognize. What are the "forbidden trees" that God does *not* want me to eat from, delve into, and research? These forbidden trees will probably not be identified by a direct word from God, but God is powerful, through the work of His Spirit, to guide us in recognizing and acknowledging them. For instance, a male researcher who wishes to improve the conditions of women in a specific community may experience a limitation on access in some cultures, due to his gender. Therefore, he will need to be keenly aware of his limitations. Another example of limitations has been brought about by COVID-19, which has definitely slowed down or limited the extent of some research projects; see for instance Felicia Ang's (2021) limitations and delimitations section in her dissertation. These limitations must be recognized and managed in humility and in community.

Write down the delimitations and limitations of your research project. As you write, remember: "The one who has knowledge uses words with restraint, and whoever has understanding is even-tempered" (Proverbs 17:27).

What's Next?

In this chapter, we have discussed the facets of defining a research problem and translating it into research questions. You are now ready to complete the first chapter of your research proposal. In the following chapter of this book, we will ponder how to ground research on solid foundations. These foundations will highly strengthen the credibility of the research undertaken.

What Questions Do You Still Have?

At the end of this chapter, perhaps you may want to brainstorm and record all the questions you might still have. What and who are the resources the Lord has made available to you to find some of the answers to these questions? Perhaps the next chapter will also provide some answers.

Chapter 3: On What Foundations Will You Build Your Research?

To establish a solid foundation and credibility for your research, we will look at how integrity is woven into finding and referencing foundational academic sources. Then, we will reflect on different elements that are crucial to writing a valuable literature review that will anchor your research meaningfully while ensuring that the reader will realize how your new research brings added value to the body of research already available.

Where Are the Sources of Life?

Figure 3: Water as One Source of Life

Source: Poland – Miedzygórze, Waterfall of Wilczki in Śnieżnik Mountains, Sudetes © Merlin, Wikimedia (CC BY-SA 3.0)

When a Samaritan woman came to draw water, Jesus said to her, "Will you give me a drink?" (His disciples had gone into the town to buy food.) The Samaritan woman said to him, "You are a Jew and I am a Samaritan woman. How can you ask me for a drink?" (For Jews do not associate with Samaritans.) Jesus answered her, "If you knew the gift of God and who it is that asks you for a drink, you would have asked him and he would have given you living water." "Sir," the woman said, "you have nothing to draw with and the well is deep. Where can you get this living water? Are you greater than our father Jacob, who gave us the well and drank from it himself, as did also his sons and his livestock?" Jesus answered, "Everyone who drinks this water will be thirsty again, but whoever drinks the water I give them will never thirst. Indeed, the water I give them will become in them a spring of water welling up to eternal life." (John 4:7–14, NIV)

As you start your research, you will need to gather information to give it a strong element of life. Where there is life, there are living cells that constantly multiply and transmit their genetic content to the new cells. In your research, you will need to account for the "genetic content" of your research, i.e. the academically recognized sources that the Lord has made available to you. You will reflect on how to read and understand such sources, and on how to use them with integrity and for Christ's glory.

How Is Your Research Guarded?

Figure 4: Overview of the Old Testament Tabernacle

Let us go back to the Old Testament worship imagery that we find in the construction of the tabernacle (Exod. 27:9–19). As worshippers were nearing the tabernacle, they saw this huge rectangular barrier surrounding all the tabernacle's elements (Figure 4). It was a white woven linen fence held up by 60 pillars and a huge multi-colored gate (which we will discuss later). From the outside, this fence established a separation between the impure outside camp of the Jewish worshipper (representing the outside world) and God's presence. From the inside, this fence acted as a surrounding or shield from the outside world. To all those who found their place inside, it became a place of protection and stability. ... It was a place where one could meet with the Living God. (Conner, 1976, p. 73)

Conner (1976) explained, "The Fine Linen is symbolic of that spotless purity of Christ" (p. 74). This contention is supported by other passages in the book of Revelation (3:4; 19:8, 11–14), for instance, where we see that Christ's righteousness and purity are imputed to those who believe in Him (1 Cor. 1:30). Thus, in our particular research journey, we should emphasize how much the integrity that we display in our research is indeed a *reflection of the purity of Christ*. It is a display of God's holiness. Consequently, our research will be guided by Christ's purity, integrity, and holiness. How shall we write with integrity?

Many videos and writings have been published on what plagiarism is and on how to write with integrity, so there is no need to address this concern further here. Our God is Truth. This is why, in the above-quoted passage from John 4, Christ works with this Samaritan woman to lead her to the real source of the life she is called to live—Christ himself. The assumption is that, like the woman at the well, Christian researchers will take the time to dialog with Christ as they reflect and write. There is abundance of joy and life in His presence when there is abundance of truth and integrity. A constant acknowledgment of one's limitations and of the contributions others have made to one's thinking, conclusions, and new conceptual frameworks—like the Samaritan woman's life-changing acknowledgment—is absolutely non-negotiable. There too, the balance between your own voice and the voices of your peers and predecessors will be found in knowing who you are in Christ, as a researcher, and acknowledging the "cloud of witnesses" (Heb. 12:1) that surrounds you.

As a Christian researcher, you are called to follow the apostle Paul's lead: "I did not shrink from declaring to you the whole counsel of God" (Acts 20:27, ESV). Paul's whole discourse to the Ephesian Christians was intended to demonstrate how integrity was woven throughout his ministry to them, in all areas of life, from the financial to the spiritual aspects. Paul follows in the steps of Christ who, in his so-called high priestly prayer, said, "And this is eternal life, that they know you, the only true God, and Jesus Christ whom you have sent. I glorified you on earth, having accomplished the work that you gave me to do" (John 17:3–4, ESV). This is a beautiful expression of Christ, linking the full accomplishment of His ministry to the only *true* God! Wouldn't each of us, as Christian researchers, like to be able to say, thoroughly and deeply before God and before humans, that we have fully and truthfully accomplished the work God has entrusted us with? Let us follow Paul's recommendation and "Do your best to present yourself to God as one approved, a worker who does not need to be ashamed and who correctly handles the word of truth" (2 Tim. 2:15, ESV). Integrity and truth will indeed bring the abundant life to which Christ refers in John 4.

On the practical side, it will be important for you to develop an organized system for keeping track of the references to all the sources you consult. Several software programs (either paid or open-source[12]) can be helpful in that regard if you want to go beyond the older tradition of keeping note cards or notebooks. This will also require a high level of discipline and organization on your part, so as not to forego a single reference. Humility and discipline are a Christian researcher's key values!

How Shall We Anchor Our Research?

To hold up that fence around the tabernacle and its linen stretches, there were 60 pillars held straight by cords, as shown in Figure 5. The aligned pillars and then the woven materials connecting the pillars were the first picture the worshipper had when approaching the tabernacle. These pillars were made of wood (probably acacia wood). Their bases were bronze and their "hoods" with the hooks were made of silver. Cords were holding the pillars solidly to the ground.

Figure 5: Pillars to Anchor Your Research

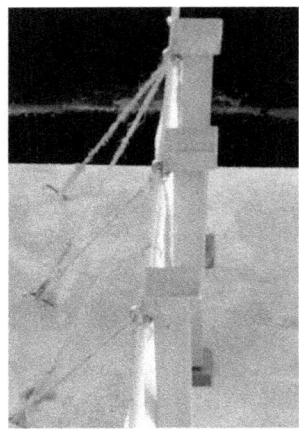

---

[12] See for example Zotero.com, Mendeley.com, or Endnote.com.

Chapter 3: On What Foundations Will You Build Your Research?

These cords were held in the ground by very strong brass hooks. The hooks were dug into the ground so that the pillar would not shake. Similarly, as you seek to enter into the core elements of your worshipful research, you first need to expose how you will anchor your research solidly in relevant conceptual or theoretical frameworks[13] that will give solid cohesion to your research.

Therefore, as you write your so-called literature review chapter (which I would rather refer to as your "worship foundations"), you will need to identify the main pillars or conceptual or theoretical frameworks supporting your research, and also the elements that will create unity around your overall research project. The conceptual frameworks or theories will give a strong academic steadiness to your research. Recall that the hooks of the tabernacle were solidly grounded in the surrounding sand or soil. Their solidity and importance were indisputable in that harsh desert environment. Likewise, it is highly advisable to use conceptual or theoretical frameworks that are relevant to your specific context. Often, in non-Western dissertations, a litany of Western conceptual frameworks is presented, but their application to non-Western contexts is flawed. In the analysis of conceptual frameworks, researchers will consider the relevance of the frameworks to their specific research focus in context, as well as the gaps or unrooted elements that these frameworks may have. This analysis will also bring forward the particular novel aspect of their research.

Just as these pillars were systematically aligned and were held straight by cords, bars, and hooks, one by one, likewise you, for each research secondary question, will need to identify the conceptual or theoretical framework(s) undergirding it. Practically, you will take your research matrix and add a column next to the first two columns with your research objectives and your research questions. It will look like Table 4.

---

[13] Throughout this guide, the terms of contextual or theoretical frameworks will be used interchangeably. *Personally, I try not to be too dogmatic, since the terms 'theoretical' and 'conceptual' have roots in the Greek (theory: speculative thought which relates to abstract thought) and Latin (conceptus: which relates to abstract thought). The essential focus is to recognize the (or rather some of our) underlying frameworks of our thought and our analysis in order to propose to humanity what God leads us to propose, while recognizing our contextual frameworks and limitations. This is why I like using the image of the weaver's frame, which clearly implies this movement from the old to the new while recognizing the limits of this movement within the previous frame (frame of the weaver). In fact, it is the VITALISTIC MOVEMENT and CREATIVITY from the old to the new that is most important and worth emphasizing while identifying where we come from and where we are going to in our thought patterns.*

Table 4: Example of a Matrix of Main Focus, Questions, and Conceptual or Theoretical Frameworks

RESEARCH FOCUS	RESEARCH QUESTION	CONCEPTUAL/ THEORETICAL FRAMEWORK (found in the references below)
Overall focus	How can doctoral students be helped to complete their doctoral dissertation?	
1st secondary	How many students have failed to complete their doctoral dissertation in the past 10 years?	Dissertation completion: No longer higher education's invisible problem*
2nd secondary	Why do students fail to complete their doctoral dissertation?	The Ph.D. experience: A review of the factors influencing doctoral students' completion, achievement, and well-being**
3rd secondary	What quality of support is provided to doctoral students?	Four-dimensional model for doctoral student support***
4th secondary	What solutions are proposed to help students complete their dissertations?	Above-referenced frameworks and Testing theories of doctoral student persistence at a Hispanic serving institution****

Sources: * S.M. Marshcal, B. Klocko and J. Davidson (2017), ** A. Sverdlik et al. (2018), *** S.C. Conceição and L. Hill (2019), **** G.S. Vaquera (2007)

This process will lead to identifying the frameworks that are relevant to each research question. You may have several frameworks to refer to for one specific research focus, just as each pillar was anchored with at least four silver hooks and cords to keep it straight. Each was pointing in a different direction. But together, they complemented each other and thus were keeping the pillar straight. As you present your frameworks, you may also want to emphasize the *direction*, i.e. the specific slant or focus, of that framework and demonstrate how it complements other frameworks. Consequently, you will appear to be making the literature *dialog* with each other. This is why the phrase "literature review" could be rephrased as *dialog with literature*, which is a much life-conveying term. This dialog will be conducted with integrity and order, but also dynamically and in a lively manner to convey the multifaceted and life-giving approaches that can support a specific focus in research. The end result will be the multicolored gate that we are going to look at next.

> As you complete your own research matrix with the relevant theoretical or conceptual frameworks, ask the Lord to open your eyes and widen your research skills to understand into what unresearched area He is guiding you, while thoroughly acknowledging where He has already preceded your work with research (frameworks) that are already available.

What a Colorful Gate!

You have walked around the walls of your research and strengthened each of its pillars, and now you come in front of a beautifully woven gate. It seals the entrance into the heart of your research. Figure 6 is a representation of this gate.

> For the entrance to the courtyard, provide a curtain twenty cubits long, of blue, purple, and scarlet yarn and finely twisted linen—the work of an embroiderer—with four posts and four bases. (Exod. 27:16)

Figure 6: The Gate of the Tabernacle

According to commentators, the divinity (blue), royalty (purple), humanity (fine linen), and sacrifice (scarlet) of the Lord Jesus are represented here (Kiene, 1976, pp. 35–38). For instance, the four gospels bring forth four different aspects of Christ's life. Through all of what He is, Christ can give us access to deeper truths. Through Him and all the interwoven beauties that He represents, we will enter more deeply into the methodological aspects of the research.

This gate can be moved and opened. It is dynamic. It opens to let the worshipper into God's more intimate presence. It allows the worshipper to enter closer to the presence of the fully living God! That is what your research calls you to do: to lead your community closer to God's presence!

To conclude, I would just like to wink at those of us who believe that the practice of the arts can be done to worship God and bring Him glory—even in the research process!

> Then Moses said to the sons of Israel, "See, the LORD has called by name Bezalel the son of Uri, the son of Hur, of the tribe of Judah. And He has filled him with the Spirit of God, in wisdom, in understanding and in knowledge and in all craftsmanship; to make designs for working in gold and in silver and in bronze, and in the cutting of stones for settings and in the carving of wood, so as to perform in every inventive work. He also has put in his heart to teach, both he and Oholiab, the son of Ahisamach, of the tribe of Dan. He has filled them with skill to perform every work of an engraver and of a designer and of an embroiderer, in blue and in purple *and* in scarlet *material,* and in fine linen, and of a weaver, as performers of every work and makers of designs." (Exod. 35:30–35, NASB)

An interesting question for researchers would be how to make visuals or audio-visual supports for an academic *dialog with literature.* Perhaps dynamic and colorful concept maps or web pages with audio recordings could be helpful. What about developing skits through which representatives of different conceptual or theoretical frameworks could present and argue their cases with each other? Academic research as an act of creative worship is not limited to written words, but is open to so many artistic expressions of worship that remain untapped![14]

What's Next?

As they went through the gates in the inner courtyard, priests had several rituals to perform. Likewise, as you enter into your research, there are a few rituals that you will need to perform, as we will see in the next chapter.

The next major step in the research process is to develop a research methodology or process that will reflect your calling to do research that

---

[14] Here is an article that may present some interesting reflections in this respect: https://www.giarts.org/article/art-as-research-art-art-research

will bring God's *shalom* to the communities you serve. This endeavor might seem to be another major challenge, but please remember Psalm 121:

> I lift up my eyes to the mountains—
> where does my help come from?
> My help comes from the Lord,
> the Maker of heaven and earth.
>
> He will not let your foot slip—
> he who watches over you will not slumber;
> indeed, he who watches over Israel
> will neither slumber nor sleep.

Therefore, we can trust our God who will watch over us, and also over those whom He has entrusted to our care.

Let Us Try to Be Creative!

Could you take a piece of research you have developed, or a literature review that you have already constructed, and transform it into an artistic piece (music, poetry, theater, drawing or painting)?

Chapter 4: What Is Your Research Approach?

By now, you have walked around the walls of your research, strengthened each of its pillars, and passed through the beautifully woven gate to enter into the outer courtyard (Figure 7).

Figure 7: The Outer Courtyard

The outer court was a large area that contained two major items: the bronze altar and the bronze laver. These were probably the most used items in the tabernacle. The outer court was the place where the Israelites brought their sacrifices to God and where the priests would slaughter these animals to offer them to God. And the priests would go to the laver to purify themselves from the blood.

Figure 8: The Bronze Altar

The bronze altar (Figure 8) was used to offer sacrifices of consecration (to God) and sacrifices of expiation (of sins). Leviticus chapters 1 through 7 describes the five types of sacrifices that could be offered (Table 5). First came the burnt offering (ch. 1), the grain or cereal offering (ch. 2), and the fellowship or peace offering (ch. 3), which were all voluntary sacrifices. Then there was the sin offering and the guilt offering (chs. 4–5), which were required sacrifices for intentional or unintentional sins. These chapters develop the rituals that the worshipper or the priest had to follow. The worshipper and the priest had to discern the reason for the offering and its purpose and make the appropriate sacrifice accordingly. Some sacrifices required animals, while others did not; therefore, much discernment was needed as to the specific sacrifice and sacrificial process required for each kind of offering.

Table 5: The Sacrifices in Leviticus

Leviticus 1	Burnt offering
Leviticus 2	Grain offering
Leviticus 3	Fellowship or peace offering
Leviticus 4–5:13	Sin offering
Leviticus 5:14–26	Guilt offering
Leviticus 6-7	Laws regarding the offerings

Likewise, as Christian researchers seek to bring their "research offering" before the Lord, they need to reflect on the reason for and the purpose of the research so as to define what the research process or approach (sacrifice) will look like. Many different research processes and approaches are possible. I would compare them to the first three kinds of offerings, which represent the expression of a pure act of thankfulness and worship to the Lord. Then, the purpose of the research approaches adopted could be compared to the last two kinds of offerings, which were designed to respond to and deal with specific or unknown sins (just as research problems are a direct consequence of specific delinquent behaviors or due to unconscious deficiencies).

What Research Approaches?

After entering through the "gate" and stepping into the "outer court," researchers must decide and clarify what research processes or approaches they want to adopt. To make that decision, clear analysis and reflection are needed. Making these decisions is often quite a challenging step for researchers. Several research approaches or processes have been presented in various research methodology books and frameworks. Figure 9 presents a model that summarizes many of them, called the Research Onion (Saunders et al., 2019, p. 208, as quoted in Seuring, Stella, & Stella, 2012). I like it because of its strong visual appeal. However, other approaches might be considered, such as appreciative inquiry, which is not included in the Research Onion. The key in deciding which research approaches to use is to clearly understand the specific features of each research approach and be able to articulate them clearly while drawing contrasts with other approaches that might not be useful. The purpose of clarifying research approaches is to demonstrate to the audiences of the research that the best methodological approaches have been chosen, in contrast to other possible approaches. A critical explanation of the choice of research processes must be clearly presented. Many novice researchers omit this piece of their work, thereby significantly weakening their research because they have not demonstrated that they have thoroughly assessed the validity of the various research approaches with regard to the specific research attempted.

Figure 9: The Research Onion

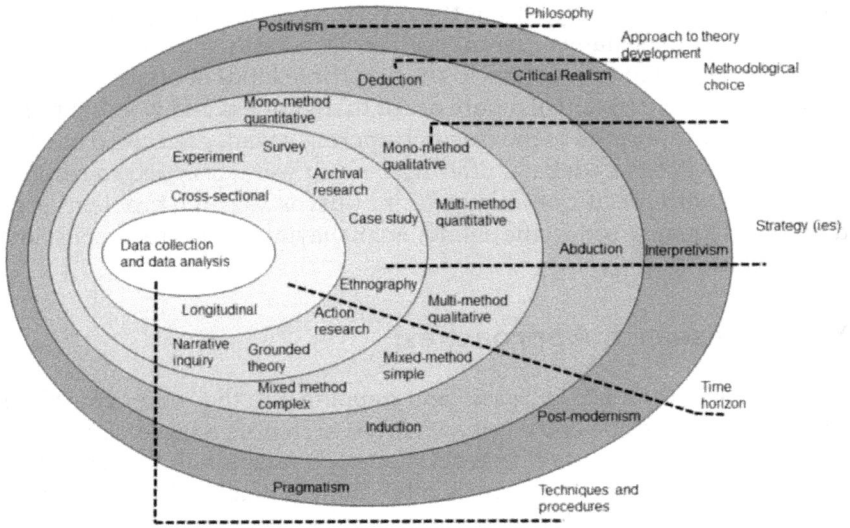

Source: Saunders N.K. et al. (2019, p. 208).

Let's take a specific example. A researcher wants to find out how to help a certain group of students who seem unable to finish their doctoral research after having worked on it for five years at a specific university. That researcher will need to decide which methodological approaches to adopt (from the choices in Saunders's Research Onion) and explain to the audience of the research why these approaches will be embraced *and* why other approaches will be rejected. In many cases, the researcher stops at the first part of the preceding sentence. For instance, the researcher might state that the mixed-methods research approach will be used because it is the "best approach to obtain the data sought."[15] But such a statement does not account for the choice of research approach. Very clear and specific arguments must be brought forward to demonstrate the need for both quantitative and qualitative research approaches. The researcher will also need to demonstrate explicitly why other approaches were considered but not selected to answer the research questions. This researcher will also have to make a case for the preferred approach by demonstrating what kind of data that specific approach will elicit which would not be possible with

---

[15] I have read similar statements numerous times in research proposals!

other research approaches. Such explanations and accountability postures are of great importance to ascertain and establish the integrity and validity of the research and will give high credibility to the researcher.

What Research Strategies?

In Old Testament Israel, once the decision was made as to the kind of sacrifice to be offered, the priest had to go through specific detailed processes to offer the sacrifice. These details are explained in Leviticus 6 and 7. For each type of sacrifice, there was a specific process to follow. The processes were not to be mixed up. Similarly, once the research approach has been determined, one must decide what specific research strategies to adopt to gather the relevant data that will answer the research questions and thus provide solutions to the research problem. The Research Onion offers many such strategies, although the list is not exhaustive; for instance, focus groups do not appear in Figure 9. Other strategies could be added to the list.

Again, the decision on research strategies has to be thoroughly argued for, in such a way as to convince the research audience that the strategies adopted are the most suitable ones in view of the research questions. Many research methodology books amply expound on the characteristics of the various research strategies.

Triangulation

A minimum of three research strategies is generally recommended to achieve *triangulation of data*. Triangulation means looking at a situation from *three angles* or perspectives. For instance, in the above-mentioned example of a researcher investigating why certain students do not complete their doctoral dissertation, a large-scale survey would permit gleaning from a substantial number of ABD (All But Dissertation) students the reasons why they did not complete their doctoral dissertation. Interviewing the dissertation supervisors from that university could be a second strategy, to gather additional perspectives on the reasons for non-completion. Third, obtaining access to these ABD students' files or exit interviews could provide another source of relevant data. Another very comprehensive example of triangulation can be found in Marco Thom's (2017) dissertation.

Data triangulation can be summarized in Figure 10. It shows that three sets of data have been obtained through the three research strategies adopted. These sets of data overlap in pairs, and each pair of the three strategies can reinforce each other. But the most reliable information is derived when all three sets of data overlap and confirm a finding.

Figure 10: Data Triangulation

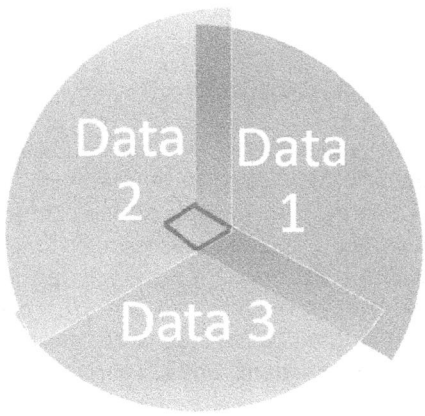

Source: Author's own construction.

The findings confirmed by all three research strategies will be the most meaningful and relevant. They will help the researcher understand the root of the problem and thus find the most appropriate solution. By the way, this figure also shows data at the periphery of the figure that represent information that is more loosely connected with the core of the problem. The data collected are never completely "clean"; that is, some data may not necessarily be helpful for research purposes. This should not be surprising, but also, these outliers may point to unanticipated or previously unconsidered issues or evidence.

The integrity and quality of the data collected are better preserved when multiple strategies are implemented. The biblical principle of Deuteronomy 19:15 and Matthew 18:16, according to which two or three witnesses are required to establish facts, is also valid in research.

Are the Research Instruments Congruent with Research Questions?

Once a research strategy is selected, the researcher will construct one or more research instruments—such as a survey, a questionnaire, an interview protocol, or focus group questions. The questions in these instruments must be very congruent with the research questions; in other words, they have to clearly help the researcher gather data that will provide answers to the research questions. Adding a column on research instruments to the research matrix, as shown in Table 6, will be helpful. The table demonstrates how the research instruments are related to specific research questions.

Table 6: Research Matrix with Research Instruments

RESEARCH FOCUS	RESEARCH QUESTION	CONCEPTUAL / THEORETICAL FRAMEWORK (found in the references below)	RESEARCH INSTRUMENTS
Main Research Focus	How can doctoral students be helped to complete their doctoral dissertation?		
1st secondary	How many students have failed to complete their doctoral dissertations in the past 10 years?	Dissertation completion: No longer higher education's invisible problem*	University documentation
2nd secondary	Why do students fail to complete their doctoral dissertations?	The Ph.D. experience: A review of the factors influencing doctoral students' completion, achievement, and well-being**	Student exit interviews (documentation)
3rd secondary	What is the quality of support provided to doctoral students?	Four-dimensional model for doctoral student support***	Interview questions 2 and 3; survey questions 6 and 7
4th secondary	What are proposed solutions to help students complete their dissertations?	Above-mentioned theories and Testing theories of doctoral student persistence at a Hispanic serving institution****	Survey questions 3, 4, 9, 11, and 12; interview questions 4 and 5

Sources: * S.M. Marshcal, B. Klocko and J. Davidson (2017), ** A. Sverdlik et al. (2018), *** S.C. Conceição and L. Hill (2019), **** G.S. Vaquera (2007)

Table 7 (a real example, used with the researcher's permission) shows how a doctoral student has made sure that the survey questions were congruent with the research questions in a red box. For each survey or interview question, the congruent research question is presented on the same line. In this way, the student can quickly determine whether all the research questions have been addressed. Furthermore, when one is analyzing the data, it will be much easier to sort the data according to the research questions. In this specific instance, the student has also color-coded the questions according to his data analysis needs before administering the survey, to make data analysis easier later on.

Table 7: Sample Survey Questions

11.	How did members of your local church feel about stopping face-to-face services? Was there any form of resistance from members?	Research Question #2: How did the Church respond to the restrictions of the COVID-19 pandemic?
12.	How did your local church maintain discipleship programs such as Bible study classes, Sunday school, prayer meetings, baptism classes, confirmation classes, etc.?	Research Question #3: What are the various components of a techno-theology for a digital church?
13.	Tell me about technology. How did your local church use technology to reach the congregants during the COVID-19 restrictions?	Research Question #3: What are the various components of a techno-theology for a digital church?
14.	What did you hear from other congregations in your neighborhood on how they navigated the challenges of the pandemic?	Research Question #3: What are the various components of a techno-theology for a digital church?
15.	Did your spiritual life grow during the pandemic? What did your church do to stay connected?	Research Question #4: How can the church review the theology of the "gathered church" while discovering a theology of the digital church?

The principle of *congruence* with the main research question and the secondary research questions is a biblical principle, which actually belongs to God's identity and creative work. The whole universe has been created by God with highly congruent systems. Our physical body is completely congruent in terms of how all the parts operate and are connected with each other. In 1 Corinthians 12, Paul demonstrates how the spiritual body, Christ's church, is completely congruent while being dependent on and connected with the head, which is Christ. Similarly, it behooves Christian researchers to pay very close attention to the various parts of the research instruments used, so that the data obtained will clearly be connected to or congruent with the research questions. The research process in the social sciences or in the business world is not just a recipe to be followed, but an organic analysis of life-related processes where God's principles of congruence and systemic approaches to life will be attested. Therefore, researchers are highly encouraged to maintain an appreciative inquiry mindset (See the appreciative inquiry section in chapter1) as they proceed with their research where they seek to identify where God has already preceded them.

Prayerfully, while seeking the Lord's inspiration and also the advice of your personal learning community, update your research matrix with your anticipated research approaches and research instruments, maintaining the congruence that you have built thus far for your research. Claim this promise of Prov. 3:6 (NLT): "Seek his will in all you do, and he will show you which path to take."

Whom Should Data Be Collected From? (Sampling)

The Hebrew worshipper had to choose the animals to be offered to God among all the animals available on the farm or in the market. Only *pure* animals could be offered to God. They were chosen according to specific criteria outlined in Leviticus 11.

Similarly, to collect data from larger groups of people according to the intent of their research, researchers must select people who adequately represent the population being studied. Most textbooks on research methods analyze this challenge and propose strategies to define samples that are relevant to the type of proposed research.[16]

The principles of *equity* and *fair representation* of the segments of the population being studied must be constantly maintained, while the re-

---

[16] See for instance Saunders (2019, chapter 7) or Robson and McKarten (2016, pp. 144, 276).

searcher also seeks to maintain awareness of one's possible biases. Furthermore, I would encourage letting the principle of *shalom* undergird the sampling strategies. The questions to be asked could sound like this one: *What groups of people will need to participate and be adequately represented in this study in order for God's shalom to fully expand in this location or situation?*

Pray through Matthew 5:9 (NIV): "Blessed are the peacemakers, for they will be called children of God." Reflect on your sampling approaches. Will they reflect God's affection for the most hidden or vulnerable people within the population being studied? How could you sampling better reflect God's heart for them?

How Do Researchers Maintain Integrity in Their Research?

We have reviewed the various practical steps, approaches, and strategies that researchers will embrace so as to collect reliable data that will affirm the credibility and validity of their research. However, researchers are fallible humans who might be personally affected by the data they collect. For instance, when interviewing subjects, they will hear some emotionally shattering stories. How can researchers preserve their own integrity and "cleanliness" as they often get very close to "dirty" findings?

Looking back to the outer court of the Old Testament tabernacle, the second main piece of furniture in the outer court was the bronze laver. We know that it was made out of bronze, but we don't know its dimensions. And we read that it was made from the women's mirrors (Ex. 38:8). According to Christine Lilyquist (1979), it is likely that these bronze mirrors were taken from the Egyptians when the Israelites were leaving Egypt, as Egyptian women had bronze mirrors. The laver was placed between the altar and the entrance to the holy place (Lev. 30:17–21).

The fact that the bronze laver was made out of Egyptian mirrors encourages researchers to use the wisdom of academic colleagues who are not necessarily Christian. The Lord has also given insight and wisdom to them. Likewise, many secular books on research methodology provide valuable information on current research perspectives and strategies. As a Christian researcher, you are highly encouraged to use these resources while asking God to guide you as to how to integrate their approaches, strategies, and implementation processes in specific parts of your research. The Holy Spirit will guide you to shape your research methods and frameworks according to His will, including the use of methodologies or approaches that may not have been initially drafted by Christian researchers. For instance, the Technology Acceptance Model seems ideologically neutral, but Freud's presuppositions and those of Critical Race Theory may not be and will need to be reshaped. God uses the people whom he wants to use for His purposes, even though they don't always realize it! As a side note, one recent trend in research methodologies is a critical examination of the challenges and opportunities of cross-cultural research.[17] Cross-cultural research is often omitted in traditional texts on research methods. With the overarching trend toward globalization of research methods and approaches, I would highly encourage you to gain awareness and understanding of perspectives on research in non-Western contexts.

Figure 11: The Bronze Laver

Cleansing was an important part of the priestly rules. The sacrifices being offered had to be clean, so the priests cleansed themselves often. We can imagine what a challenge this may have been as the animals were slaughtered and blood was splashing all over the place! Even before starting their work as priests, they had to be completely bathed in an act of consecration to God at the bronze laver (Figure 11). What does this say to the researcher?

Priests had to wash themselves once completely during their initial consecration service. This washing could be treated as analogous to the researcher's initial initiation to research methodologies, including courses on research methods, accompanied by exercises, projects, and reflections. Christian researchers offer themselves to God as they put their faith in Christ and surrender their lives to Him. They seek to present an adequate

---

[17] See, for instance, Pranee Lianputtong (2022), Linda Miller Cleary (2013), and Fons J. R. van de Vijver (2021).

proposal to their research department, which is the initial step in the university's validation of the research.

However, priests also had to return to the laver constantly throughout the day as they continued the process of offering sacrifices to God. This constant movement reminds us of Romans 12:1–2, which urges Christians, including Christian researchers, to offer themselves to God and to allow the constant renewing of their minds through the work of the Holy Spirit (2 Cor. 3:16) and the word of God (Col. 3:16). As they move back and forth in the different research processes, researchers will need to check in constantly with God and assess their thoughts, attitudes, and emotions, as well as the reliability and ethical viability of their research.

Search me, God, and know my heart;
test me and know my anxious thoughts.

See if there is any offensive way in me,
and lead me in the way everlasting. (Ps. 139:23–24, NIV)

What is the "everlasting way" that the Holy Spirit is putting on your heart as you reflect on your integrity as a researcher? Write your thoughts prayerfully in your personal research journal.

This last perspective (ethical viability) represents an area that has been very strongly promoted in research processes in recent decades. Christian researchers should pay the utmost respect to each human being, created in the image of God himself. Furthermore, researchers are also called to steward the earth with which the Lord has entrusted us, using it in ways that will not damage the reputation of or discredit any fellow human being. Most universities maintain an Institutional Review Board (IRB), which initially was driven by humanistic motivations. However, Christian researchers have deeper motives that undergird their research attempts. Therefore, they should be role models with regard to the ethics that guide their collection and handling of data.

Another application of the constant need to "go to the laver" is that researchers with intellectual integrity will avoid plagiarism in every way possible. Although researchers may be deeply immersed in their readings and may tend to adopt phrases or thoughts that they have read, they will be careful to cite and reference the thoughts taken from others as thoroughly as possible. Plagiarism checkers are available to students at most institutions. Each time researchers cite and reference a quote, they should "go to the laver" and acknowledge their own integrity before the Lord.

Constant sanctification in God's presence is a non-negotiable item for Christian researchers!

What's Next?

We have looked at the two main items of the outer courtyard and reflected on the decisions that researchers will make as they develop their research plans. The time has come to actually do field research and put the research plan into concrete practice. Throughout the period of data gathering, what are the important elements that the Christian researcher should remember? The next chapter turns to that question.

What Is Your Worshipful Response?

As you conclude this stage of your study, write (or express by some other creative means) a prayer to God that articulates what He has put on your heart as you have reflected on the various research approaches and strategies that you anticipate using in your research.

Chapter 5: Gathering and Analyzing Data

The time used while data are gathered is a special time. It is a time of high-level interaction with the communities under study. Different emotions may grab the Christian researcher during that period: joy, surprise, astonishment as data are uncovered, but also discouragement, frustration, or disorientation when processes move in different directions than anticipated.

I would like to propose to Christian researchers that this time of data gathering is, foremost, a sacred time when you, like the priests officiating in the tabernacle, enter into the Holy Place of God's presence. The anchor that will keep you grounded during that period often marked by strong emotions will be your closeness with your God while realizing the sacredness of the data that you have collected. These data will allow you to complete your research as an offering to God and as a response to God's missional call on your life. So let us reflect on what the Holy Place (Figure 12) in the tabernacle looked like to find out how a more intimate and close relationship with our Triune God can sustain you during this special time in the research process.

Figure 12: The Holy Place

Feeling Overwhelmed?

The walls of the Holy Place were extremely high, about 4.57 meters or 15 feet. At first, priests may have felt overwhelmed as they entered into this space. As you seek to enter into God's Holy Place, and as you feel overwhelmed by all the data and elements involved in your research, realize that God's presence is so much larger, wider, deeper, and higher than what you can think or imagine.

Let us sing to and worship our God with this song while proclaiming His greatness: https://www.youtube.com/watch?v=PP9BjKnDaFk. Our God is also extremely powerful and willing to walk with you in this sacred and perhaps overwhelming place where you uncover data for your research.

Priests had to enter into the Holy Place at least twice a day to ensure that the incense and the lights were burning, and they replaced the bread once a week. Thus, they were in constant interaction with God's presence, day in and day out. Similarly, each Christian researcher must take the time to enter into God's presence and *present* Him with your data that you are about to collect or have just collected. One way to do that could be to keep a research reflection journal that you update daily and that you actually present to the Lord, day in and day out.

I cannot resist quoting this powerful passage from 1 Corinthians 1:26–30 (NIV):

> Brothers and sisters, think of what you were when you were called. Not many of you were wise by human standards; not many were influential; not many were of noble birth. But God chose the foolish things of the world to shame the wise; God chose the weak things of the world to shame the strong. God chose the lowly things of this world and the despised things—and the things that are not—to nullify the things that are, so that no one may boast before him. It is because of him that you are in Christ Jesus, who has become for us wisdom from God—that is, our righteousness, holiness and redemption.

As we realize our incapacity and lack of wisdom, our limitations (physical or intellectual), and the apparent lack of recognition and worth that our research may appear to have according to human standards, let us realize that *because of God, we are hidden in Jesus Christ,* and that He is our *wisdom,* our *holiness,* and our *redemption.* He will give us the wisdom to conduct data collection and to interpret the data. His holiness will guard us from any wickedness encountered in the data collection journey. His redemption

Chapter 5: Gathering and Analyzing Data 73

will, through His Holy Spirit, guide us to propose innovative and redemptive approaches to collecting and analyzing data. Spending time in God's presence will sustain you throughout the challenges of data collection and interpretation phases of your research. It is time invested wisely!

Who Is Our Constant Guide and Safeguard?

In the tabernacle's Holy Place, there were three main pieces of furniture: the table of the showbread, the candlestick of pure gold with seven lamps, and the golden altar of incense. Figure 13 (with the eastern and western walls removed) gives a clearer picture of where things were located in relationship to the two curtains, the one on the left (south side, the exit to the outer court) and the one on the right (north side, the entrance to the Most Holy Place). The Holy Place was a very peaceful place where the priests checked the level of the oil each morning and evening, bringing in burning coal and pouring incense over it.

Figure 13: Overall Picture of the Holy Place

Besides all the symbolic meaning of these three elements that are amply documented in many commentaries, as we specifically focus on the activities of Christian researchers, let us reflect on some lessons that may be learned from the Holy Place as to the various aspects of or perspectives on the data gathering phase of research.

How Does the Holy Spirit Support Our Research Work?

As we gather data, our Triune God accompanies us throughout, although it may require discernment to recognize this. The golden candlestick with its lamps and burning oil (Figure 14) can represent God's support of our research through the light shed by the Holy Spirit. The dimensions of this candlestick are unknown, but one can assume that it was quite large to illuminate the whole Holy Place. The priests had to light and replenish the lamps of the golden candlestick with oil each morning and evening. Likewise, you are strongly encouraged to take the time each morning and evening (and throughout the day!) to direct your thoughts toward the Holy Spirit who wants to constantly fill them! The Holy Spirit will work with you to illuminate areas, even very dark ones, which need to be uncovered during your data collection efforts.

Figure 14: The Golden Candlestick

Remember the Lord's words that "the Father ... will give you another advocate to help you and be with you forever—the Spirit of truth. ... But you know him, for he lives with you and will be in you" (John 14:16–17, NIV). We have this wonderful assurance that the Holy Spirit, the Spirit of Truth, lives in us now! As a consequence, as Christian researchers, we need to heed Paul's recommendation to "Guard the good deposit that was entrusted to you—guard it with the help of the Holy Spirit who lives in us" (2 Timothy 1:14, NIV). We have to *guard* the specific research area and data with which the Lord has entrusted us. This guarding entails a constant effort to *steward* the new discoveries we may be making in our data gathering efforts through the power and discernment of the Holy Spirit. Let us bring them constantly into the light of God's presence and recognize the work of the Holy Spirit in directing us, sometimes unexpectedly (as symbolized by the lack of measurements of the candlestick), toward the data that God wants us to acknowledge and work with!

As we interpret the data collected, we are called to remain under the guidance of the Holy Spirit. Our Lord promised us that the Holy Spirit will guide us "into all truth" (John 16:13, NLV). The purpose of our research is to find the additional truth that God wants to reveal to us so that we can become agents of His *shalom* as a consequence of that revelation. This takes time. The Spirit *guides* us into all truth, which means that growth and time are involved. It is not necessarily a sudden revelation but a step-by-step understanding as we live with Him and touch base with Him each morning and evening—i.e. throughout our research work, especially during the data collection and analysis phases. Again, we need special divine insights and enlightenment to discover the truth God has called us to find through this specific research effort. Eventually, *all* that God has called us to find and discover will be fully revealed and brought to light by the Holy Spirit as we keep working with perseverance and resilience in His presence.

 As you are entering deeper into the light of God's truth through the Holy Spirit guiding you in your research, do you allow yourself to be regulated by Him and completely filled by Him? In your personal research journal, jot down some thoughts or a response prayer.

How Do We Deal with Our Humanity?

Another piece of furniture in the Holy Place was the "table of the showbread." The bread shown in Figure 15 was the result of an experiment conducted following the actual ingredient measurements given by God to Moses.[18] It looks a bit different from the nice loaves of bread we often find in other tabernacle pictures. The supporting table was made of acacia wood and covered with gold. Two rows of six loaves each were put on it. The bread was made of specific quantities of fine flour (i.e. wheat crushed into powder) that was baked in fire (Lev. 24:5-9). Each of these loaves looked may have looked different. Finally, frankincense was to be put on these breads. Besides preventing the loaves from molding as the bread was sitting there for a week, it would also provide an aroma in the Holy Place. The priests were to change the bread each Sabbath and eat the old bread in the Holy Place. How can this image encourage Christian researchers?

---

[18] This way of portraying the showbread seems to conform better to the biblical specifications that refer to rows and not stacks of bread, in contrast to most other pictures of the table of the showbread.

Figure 15: The Table of the Showbread

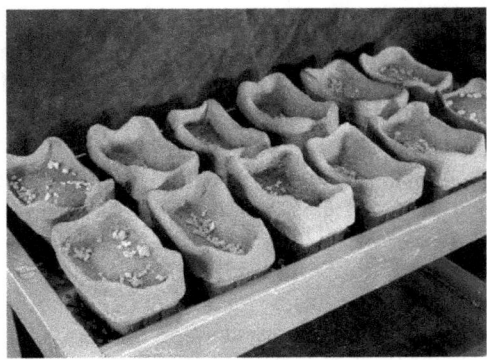

Source: https://www.freebibleimages.org/photos/sh-show-bread/

In this description, we can find two instances of references to our humanity (and commentators also refer to Christ's humanity). The acacia wood and the flour both come from living plants. To obtain the wood or the flour, the plant has to die. The wood has to be cut and the flour crushed. We cannot help but recall these words of our Lord: "For sure, I tell you, unless a seed falls into the ground and dies, it will only be a seed. If it dies, it will give much grain" (John 12:24, NLV).

First of all, doing research as part of God's calling will imply death in some way in your life: death to some social life or relationships, some dreams that you had for that part of your life, or maybe even the dreams you had for your research! As you gather data, you may find that the field data do not correspond to what you expected; your hopes may be crushed and you may have to start again! Or you may think that you have done a good job of writing up your data but your supervisor tells you to start all over again; so much time lost (dead). Bread put on a table built with human effort is not worthless. Just as the table is covered by gold, God's life is lived through you and covers you. Furthermore, just as the loaves are covered by frankincense to protect them from degradation, as you "dwell in the shelter of the Most High [you] will rest in the shadow of the Almighty" (Psalm 91:1, NIV) and God's Spirit will protect you from the ruining of your research efforts.

As a researcher, you have research protocols, plans, and a detailed timeline that you may have submitted to your research supervisor. But as you collect data, you encounter in many ways the unpredictability of life and of people, as well as your own humanity. People whom you are scheduled to interview may not show up, so you have to find new interviewees. Or surveys that you send out are not returned. Or you get sick and have to reschedule some of your field data collection. Or a war breaks out and you cannot collect any data from that region anymore. Or ... (you can fill in whatever outcomes you are encountering). Your "loaves of bread" are irregular, but God will make them fit in the whole scheme of the "table," i.e. the whole scheme of the research He wants you to complete. Here is a promise that we can rely on during distressful and unanticipated changes: "Commit to the Lord whatever you do, and he will establish your plans" (Prov. 16:3, NIV). And we can, by faith, worship our Lord together with the following prayer as we trust Him.

I encourage you to pray with the apostle Paul: "Now to him who is able to do immeasurably more than all we ask or imagine, according to his power that is at work within us, to him be glory in the church and in Christ Jesus throughout all generations, for ever and ever! Amen" (Ephesians 3:20-21).

The bread had to be changed once a week, on the Sabbath. It became the food that the priest could enjoy in God's presence that day. I wonder if this is not also an invitation to researchers to take the time to celebrate weekly Sabbaths during the months when they do their research. I have seen so many researchers working day and night on their project and becoming consumed by it, instead of following the lead that the priestly schedule offers us here. Take the time to chew the bread in God's presence. Worshipping him during our scheduled Sabbaths is of prime importance for several reasons. It is a creational institution—even God stopped his creative work on the Sabbath. We can also imagine the priests taking time to chew their bread and discuss the happenings of the week. Likewise for us, resting and stepping back will allow reflection on the progress made in the past week, prayer and worship, discussions with your support groups, etc., and it will permit the Holy Spirit to give you new insights. Why not resolve that you will not open your computer one day a week? Why not commit to observing the Sabbath in a way that provides weekly refreshment and worship time? Here is another promise that we may hold on to:

*If you keep your feet from breaking the Sabbath
and from doing as you please on my holy day,
if you call the Sabbath a delight
and the Lord's holy day honorable,
and if you honor it by not going your own way
and not doing as you please or speaking idle words,
then you will find your joy in the Lord,*

*and I will cause you to ride in triumph on the heights of the land
and to feast on the inheritance of your father Jacob. (Isa. 58:13-14)*

What Is the Role of Prayer in Research?

The last piece of furniture in the Holy Place is the altar of incense. It was a square table, higher than the table of the showbread. Like the table, it was made of acacia wood plated with gold and was surrounded by a golden crown (Figure 16). It was placed just before the veil with the cherubim that allowed entrance into the Most Holy Place (see Figure 13). Priests were to bring burning coal from the bronze altar in the outer court, place it on top of the altar of incense, and then pour over it the incense that they had carefully prepared according to the recipe God had given them (Exod. 30:1–9, 34–38).

Figure 16: The Altar of Incense

How can this image of the altar of incense encourage the Christian researcher? Like the table of the showbread, it was made of acacia wood and plated with gold. Our humanity and Christ's life in us are again portrayed here. God sees only Christ in us (Col. 1:27). As the altar of incense was placed right before the entrance to the Holiest Place, it was the piece of furniture closest to God's presence. How do we, as Christian researchers, realize most closely or intensely that we are in God's presence? Isn't that when we communicate with God in our times of prayer?

Chapter 5: Gathering and Analyzing Data

You may want to pray this prayer with the psalmist:

I call to you, LORD, come quickly to me;
hear me when I call to you.
May my prayer be set before you like incense;
may the lifting up of my hands be like the evening sacrifice. (Ps. 141:1-2, NIV)

Revelation 8:2–4 confirms that the prayers of the saints are represented by the incense brought before God. This passage also shows the incredible importance of the prayers of the saints. Leviticus 16:2 shows us that the fire to be placed on the altar of incense was to be taken from the altar of the burnt offerings. Symbolically, this shows that prayers can be brought before God only if they have been purified by the blood of Christ shed on the cross (symbolized by the altar of burnt offerings). God delights in the prayers that grow out of a heart purified by Christ's blood.

Prayer is an integral part of your research process as a Christian researcher, especially during the time of data gathering and analysis. Integrity will lead you to examine your life and clear it of anything that is not qualified for God's presence. The image of the burning fire reminds us that Christ went through the burning fire of God's wrath against sin (e.g. Ps. 22). It can thus represent this desire that we read in Psalm 51:10 (NIV): "Create in me a pure heart, O God, and renew a steadfast spirit within me." And this statement by David is a strong warning for each of us: "The Lord will not hear me if I hold on to sin in my heart" (Ps. 66:18, NLV).

God, be merciful to me! Take out of my life anything that is polluting me and interfering with my ability to relate to people or to hear your voice. Put your finger on it and I will renounce it. All I want to follow you. (Nussbaum, 2007, p. 13)

As we continue to reflect on the meaning of the incense brought before God through prayer and worship as expressed in Psalm 141 quoted above, we realize that prayer envelops and sustains every aspect of our research, especially during field research when we may be beset by so many different challenges. As Nussbaum (2007) stated, "Prayer and research are not substitutes for each other" (p. 14). The work of a Christian researcher is not a purely academic exercise. It is an exercise of faith, in response to God's calling on your life to participate in developing God's *shalom* in the specific area where you have been called to do research. Thus, your personal prayer life and constant communication with the triune God will be the atmosphere you will breathe, just as the priests of old breathed the incense while doing their duties in the Holy Place. Every aspect, every step, every encounter, and every development need to be breathed and experienced in this atmosphere of constant delight and rest in God's presence. What a blessing! We actually can live our research in God's presence!

Below, I offer two scholar's prayers, one from older times and one that is more recent. They might help you in your prayer life. The first one comes from H. C. G. Moule (1841–1920) and expresses this consecration to do all scholarly work for God's glory, as a sweet fragrance for Him.

> Lord and Savior, true and kind,
> Be the Master of my mind;
> Bless, and guide, and strengthen still
> All my powers of thought and will.
>
> While I ply the scholar's task,
> Jesus Christ, be near, I ask;
> Help the memory, clear the brain,
> Knowledge still to seek and gain.
>
> Here I train for life's swift race;
> Let me do it in Thy grace;
> Here I arm me for life's fight;
> Let me do it in Thy might.
>
> Thou hast made me mind and soul;
> I for Thee would use the whole;
> Thou hast died that I might live;
> All my powers to Thee I give.
>
> Striving, thinking, learning, still,
> Let me follow thus Thy will,
> Till my whole glad nature be
> Trained for duty and for Thee.

The following prayer is an adaptation of the Lord's Prayer regarding scholarly work. It was composed in 2018 by Deryck Chan, who graduated in 2020 with a Ph.D. in geotechnical engineering.

> Our Father in heaven, let us honour you in all our plans, all our toil, and all our achievements.
>
> Let us seek your glory and follow your commands above all else.
>
> In all our experiments into the unknown, let not our assumptions, but your will be shown.

Give us the wisdom, the intelligence, and the resources we need to carry out our work.

Forgive us of our mistakes and help us forgive ourselves and our co-workers of every mistake.

Protect us from jealousy and endue us with a heart of appreciation, so that we shall celebrate the achievements of our competitors and ourselves alike.

Lead us away from the temptations and pressures of this world to conform to malpractice, and keep us on the narrow path of integrity even when it may appear to hurt our career prospects.

For you sustain the laws of the universe for us to discover, you alone can forgive sins, and you enable us to find satisfaction in our discoveries.

Let us give all glory to you for your holy name. Amen.

You might want to print these prayers and pray them in the morning as you enter your work space, or in the evening when you close your academic work for the day. Or perhaps you may want to write your own scholar's prayer!

Although Aaron, the High Priest, was leading the work in the Holy Place, he had a team of priests supporting him in his duties. Likewise, you are not alone in your holy research duties. As you go before the Lord, day in and day out, to bring to Him your research-related work and challenges, please remember that you have a team praying with you and for you. At Bakke Graduate University where I presently serve, we require each doctoral student to have a personal learning community whose duty is not only to support the student with advice and academic support, but also to commit to praying for the student. I find this support to be of primary importance, because doing scholarly research with the Lord to extend His *shalom* here on earth will face opposition by the evil one and thus a spiritual battle is also going on. Bringing your worship before God, not only by yourself but also surrounded by a team of worshippers and intercessors, will give so much more strength and protection to your research work!

What's Next?

In this phase of your research, you have gathered your data and worked on analyzing your findings. During this often-stressful time, you have found rest in the intimacy of God's presence in the Holy Place. There you have realized how the Holy Spirit (symbolized by the candlestick) has enlightened the different steps of your data collection and given you very new thoughts while you were analyzing your data. You have also realized that although your data may not be as clean and predictable as you anticipated, you could lay them before the Lord, and that He has shown you how to preserve the data and make them congruent with your research purposes (as illustrated by the table of the showbread). You have spent quite a bit of time with the Lord, day in and day out, to find rest in His presence and bring Him the worship that comes out of your heart as you delight in Him. Now, it is time to pull your research together and finalize it so that you can bring it as your act of worship to God in the Holiest Place! The next chapter will guide you to the entrance of the Holiest Place of God's presence in the tabernacle.

Can You Count Your Blessings?

You probably are familiar with this well-known refrain from the hymn "Count Your Blessings" by Johnson Oatman (1897):

> Count your blessings, name them one by one;
> Count your blessings, see what God hath done;
> Count your blessings, name them one by one;
> Count your many blessings, see what God hath done.

Why don't you sing it now?
https://youtu.be/Hb4JBNDWhOA

I would encourage you to take a sheet of paper, your computer, your paintbrush, or any creative method and *count*—i.e. list or represent—all the *many* blessings you have experienced during the data gathering and analysis phase. Note what may have seemed to be very small and almost unnoticeable ways in which the Lord has blessed, encouraged, and helped you! Bring this summary to the altar of incense as a sweet offering to God and share it with your personal learning community members and/or your dissertation committee.

Chapter 6: Getting Ready for the Final Offering!

By now, you have completed your data collection and analysis. During that process, you have come to understand so much better the problem you researched, and you were able to answer each of your specific research questions. You have gained some very insightful understanding of the causes of your research problem and have grown in your appreciation of God's perspective on the research problem you identified, as well as of His support throughout the field research processes. You are getting ready to move one step forward.

You are now putting all your research together and preparing to cross through the final *veil*, the one that separated the Holy Place from the Holiest Place where, in Old Testament times, God manifested His utmost presence.

Figure 17: Two Views of the Veil of the Holiest Place

May I propose that this most beautiful veil (Figure 17) represents the concluding chapter(s) as well as the final putting together of your doctoral dissertation? Exodus 26:31–33 tells us that the veil was woven with fine linen and included three different colors: blue, purple, and scarlet. It was square. The linen had been brought out of Egypt, which was very well known for its fine linen—a gentle reminder that although books on research methods may not have been written by Christian researchers, they contain excellent material from which you can benefit! The spiritual meaning of the colors has been amply discussed.[19] Let us rather focus on the finished look of the veil, i.e. on finalizing your dissertation with excellence.

This veil was very finely hand-woven and must have been a very special piece of art (Exodus 26:31). The colors as they were added, the design including the cherubim, and the size had to be completely congruent and harmonious. All the elements of the veil needed to be complete and to match the required size and design. Similarly, when completing your dissertation, you will need to ensure that your concluding chapter loops back to the initial research questions, clarifying the responses to each question. In many cases, especially when you have sought to do action and transformational research, the outcomes of your action research or pilot project will be described in your concluding chapter, where you will propose the next steps or offer clear and concrete recommendations.

Then, thorough editing and formatting will be needed. I highly recommend that you secure other editors besides yourself. It is difficult to find your own mistakes. In the Old Testament, the weavers weaved the veil as a team. You should put together a team of readers and editors, and then lead that team!

As you finish the editing and the formatting of your dissertation, I encourage you to use a checklist similar to Table 8 (adapted from the Bakke Graduate University checklist) that you can adjust to your own research focus and your university requirements.

---

[19] See for instance Paul F. Kiene, (1977).

Table 8: Dissertation Review Checklist

Dissertation Review Checklist
Abstract
There is a concise summary of<ul><li>the project's purpose,</li><li>a transformational intervention approach, and</li><li>the findings.</li></ul>(300 words maximum).
Introduction Chapter
Statement of the Problem is clear, realistic, insightful, and well documented. The section<ul><li>starts with a concise statement of the issue,</li><li>indicates samples of studies related to the problem, and</li><li>indicates the significance of this particular project in view of previous similar studies or projects.</li></ul>
Context of the Problem is clear and relevant, describing<ul><li>the people (history, worldview, values, beliefs, demography, etc.),</li><li>other local contextual facts that shed light on the problem addressed (location, geography, infrastructure, etc.),</li><li>the current situation as related to the problem, and</li><li>the primary stakeholders related to this project and the intended audience for the project report.</li></ul>The chapter begins with an introductory paragraph.
Statement of Purpose is clear with<ul><li>an introductory statement of project intent, concluding with a summary of the theoretical framework of the project (the constructs, concepts, and practitioner approaches being applied in the project);</li><li>a primary research question followed by supporting questions that relate to understanding the existence of the current problem and possible solutions, conceptual components that need to be re-</li></ul>

searched to effectively address the problem, and theological issues related to the problem and solutions; and

- a summary of a transformational strategy implemented (a detailed description will be in the research methodology chapter 3 and results chapter 4).

The *Transformational Significance* section provides discussion of

- how the project improves people's lives, communities, organizations and other cultural matters, and
- how the project demonstrates transformational leadership perspectives.

The *Assumptions and Worldview* section provides

- a discussion of the author's preconceived assumptions and worldview that possibly affected project, and
- possible biases of the author that need to be honestly stated.

The *Definitions* section includes key words and terms that are relevant to the project.

Delimitations and Limitations of the project are described including

- a rationale for possibly selecting only some aspects of a problem, and
- a description of limited sample size, barriers to collecting data, limited funding, site issues, etc.

The chapter begins with an introductory paragraph and ends with a section summarizing key chapter ideas and concluding with a transition sentence that introduces the next chapter.

Literature Review: Conceptual or Theoretical Frameworks

1. *Introductory paragraph* clearly describing the conceptual or theoretical frameworks of the project, including relevant topics such as community development approaches, business models, organizational assessment strategies, and biblical foundations. This paragraph concludes with a statement of the main topics, which are generally the subheadings of the various chapter sections.
2. Chapter is *organized thematically* with relevant literature discussed in each section. The themes pertain to each of the research questions.

3. Chapter includes good representation of literature *generated from authors within the student's context*. The sections show good integration of relevant conceptual models, principles from various disciplines, and relevant biblical principles.
4. Chapter ends with *conclusions paragraph* that clearly summarizes how the various biblical and conceptual components relate to the project, along with a transition to the next chapter.

Research Methodology and Transformational Strategies

1. Chapter begins with good introductory paragraph introducing reader to the research, listing the main research question, and summarizing the transformational strategies implemented.
2. Research method(s) are
   - clearly defined using definitions from respected sources in research methodology showing how methods differ, and
   - discuss why the selected methods are best suited to answering the research questions for the project.
3. Sampling methods
   - are clearly described with rationale indicated,
   - are appropriate for answering the research questions with adequate representation of the population studied based on the research method being used, and
   - include the number of participants with demographic information included such as age range, gender, socio-economic factors, educational backgrounds, etc.
4. *Data gathering strategies* are clearly identified with purposes and rationales for each. Several data gathering strategies should be included to increase the validity of the research.
5. The *Ethical Issues* section includes information on any vulnerable populations involved, sensitive information, IRB agreement and use of consent forms when required.
6. *The practical, transformational strategy* includes
   - good planning,
   - detailed descriptions of the action steps used to implement the plan, and

	• clear discussion of how this strategy relates to the problem statement and how it is designed to bring about transformation in a community, organization, culture, etc.
7.	Appropriate *evaluation methods* are utilized to determine the validity of collected data using triangulation whenever possible. The effectiveness of the transformational strategy is evaluated based on thoroughly analyzed feedback from participants and observations of the researcher/facilitator of the project.
8.	The chapter ends with a summary paragraph and provides the reader with a transition to the next chapter.

Findings and Results

1. *Results of data collection* are clearly demonstrated using methods such as tables, charts, and graphs to clearly display findings with in-depth analysis.
2. *Results of the transformational strategy* are clearly described in detail showing how the strategy has contributed to transformation.
3. *Results of evaluation methods* include discussion of:
    - methods used for evaluation,
    - validity of data collected with triangulation, and
    - a clear indication of how people, communities, and/or organizations were transformed through the project.
4. The chapter begins with an introductory paragraph and ends with a paragraph summarizing the findings in a generalized way. The paragraph ends with a sentence that provides the reader with a transition into the next chapter.

Discussion and Conclusions

The *discussion* chapter includes:

1. the interpretation of findings and transformational strategies in relation to effectively addressing the problem,
2. the summary of validity and trustworthiness of the project,
3. the significance and implications such as
    - personal/professional/cultural insights
    - theological insights

- effective communication
- strategies discovered
- replicability of the project
- role of the student's personal learning community, and
4. recommendations and specific future action steps.
   The chapter begins with an introductory paragraph and ends with a concluding statement summarizing the project.

Mechanics of Writing

- Chapters are logically organized using relevant subheadings, introductory and summary statements, and a professional writing format. APA is preferred in the field of social sciences.
- There is evidence of critical thinking with logical academic arguments that include claims, reasons, reliable documentation, and discussion of opposing claims, utilizing culturally relevant sources from expert scholars and practitioners.
- At least one-third of the documentation is provided from sources generated within the student's context.
- The writing uses correct grammar, punctuation, and spelling with well-organized sentences that clearly communicate the intended meaning.
- There is appropriate documentation throughout the project, using reliable sources with no plagiarism.

Professional Practitioner Standards

- Discussion of data demonstrates ethical protection of human subjects.
- Overall focus of the project demonstrates the culmination and results of the student's educational process at BGU with practical, culturally relevant implementation of holistic, transformational leadership principles.

A symbolic feature of the tabernacle, and thus also of the veil, is that everything was transportable. The veil (like many parts of the tabernacle) was hung with rods and pillars so that it could be dismantled and taken to the next stop in the Israelites' pilgrimage. We do not know anything about the weight of the veil. However, it was quite large, about 4.5 meters on each side. It displayed an expression of the beauty of God's presence.

Similarly, the doctoral research you have just completed may be quite large. However, it is an expression of how you have understood something new about God's beauty in a specific context or community and have sought to convey it to that community through life-giving insights, recommendations, and perhaps action plans or proposed future projects. Your dissertation is a physical and artistic expression of the understanding and insights you have received from God throughout the unfolding of your research project.

Consequently, and as much as your university allows you to do so, you may seek to include in your dissertation a variety of expressions of your research. It does not necessarily have to be a 300-page document containing only written text! Other artistic expressions of your dissertation might include photos, links to recordings, videos, or, even better, electronic portfolios[20] that you have assembled for the purpose of your research. I love it when researchers propose creative, dynamic, and life-giving expressions of their research!

What a privilege it is, as it was for the artists weaving the veil, to communicate to the world, and specifically to your community, your calling to collaborate with God in expanding His mission and His shalom! What expressions of your creative artistic representations or artifacts could you include in your dissertation or its appendices?

What's Next?

I hope this chapter has encouraged you to review, edit, and finalize your dissertation while reflecting on what you have learned about God and your community during the research process. Although you have not forgotten the challenges encountered during the way, you will also remember how God has intervened over and over again, speaking directly to you or using other people or circumstances around you.

Now it is time to put the last full stop on your work. Lift it up to God so that you can follow Samuel's lead (1 Sam. 7:12): "Samuel then took a large stone and placed it between the towns of Mizpah and Jeshanah. He named it Ebenezer (which means 'the stone of help'), for he said, 'Up to this point the LORD has helped us!'"

---

[20] Here are some reflections on e-portfolios: Hinojosa, J. and Howe, T.-H. (2016), Walland, E. and Sahw, S (2022).

Chapter 6: Getting Ready for the Final Offering!

The final chapter will discuss your offering of your completed work to God—and to your community!

How Will You Express Your Worship to the Lord?

Select one or more worship songs that come to your mind and heart as you reflect on God's pleasure in your research, and take time out to sing them before Him! Or write your own songs of thankfulness and worship to Him.

Chapter 7: In God's Presence

We are now entering into God's Holiest Place (Figure 18), the place where his very presence is revealed and made palpable in human terms. Scripture describes the main piece of furniture that was in this place, the Ark of the Covenant:

> They shall make an ark of acacia wood; two cubits and a half shall be its length, a cubit and a half its breadth, and a cubit and a half its height. And you shall overlay it with pure gold, within and without shall you overlay it, and you shall make upon it a molding of gold round about. And you shall cast four rings of gold for it and put them on its four feet, two rings on the one side of it, and two rings on the other side of it. You shall make poles of acacia wood, and overlay them with gold. And you shall put the poles into the rings on the sides of the ark, to carry the ark by them. The poles shall remain in the rings of the ark; they shall not be taken from it. And you shall put into the ark the testimony which I shall give you. Then you shall make a mercy seat of pure gold; two cubits and a half shall be its length, and a cubit and a half its breadth. And you shall make two cherubim of gold; of hammered work shall you make them, on the two ends of the mercy seat. Make one cherub on the one end, and one cherub on the other end; of one piece with the mercy seat shall you make the cherubim on its two ends. The cherubim shall spread out their wings above, overshadowing the mercy seat with their wings, their faces one to another; toward the mercy seat shall the faces of the cherubim be. And you shall put the mercy seat on the top of the ark; and in the ark you shall put the testimony that I shall give you. There I will meet with you, and from above the mercy seat, from between the two cherubim that are upon the ark of the testimony, I will speak with you of all that I will give you in commandment for the people of Israel. (Exod. 25:10–22, RSV)

The Ark of the Covenant is an essential piece of the Holiest Place and is referred to 180 times in the Bible—which certainly confirms its importance! Many commentaries have examined its meaning and that of the mercy seat. Hebrews 9:3–5 reveals to us the content of the Ark: a golden container with manna inside, Aaron's rod that budded, and the tables of the covenant that God had given to Moses on the mountain (Heb. 5:3–5).

The only other element that was constantly present in the Holiest Place was the book of the law that God had required to be placed next to the Ark of the Covenant:

When Moses had finished writing the words of this law in a book, to the very end, Moses commanded the Levites who carried the ark of the covenant of the LORD, "Take this book of the law, and put it by the side of the ark of the covenant of the LORD your God, that it may be there for a witness against you." (Deut. 31:24–26, RSV)

Figure 18: The Holiest Place

The High Priest would come into this place once a year, the day of Yom Kippur, surrounded with a cloud of burning incense taken from the altar of incense, to sprinkle blood from the sin offering on the east side of the mercy seat (Lev. 16:11–14). The Israelites and the team of priests waited outside until the High Priest came out, having made the atonement for the sins of the people of Israel. This was a very powerful and awesome ceremony!

Going In ...

After you have completed your research, written your dissertation, and gone through all the review processes required by your university, you will come to this awesome (and stressful!) moment where you defend your research and its outcomes in front of a panel of senior researchers. Often, family and friends attend physically or via Zoom. After the jury's deliberation, there is a public announcement that you have met the academic requirements to be recognized as a *doctor*. Indeed, this is the very special moment in your life where you finalize the offer of your dissertation research to God.

Chapter 7: In God's Presence

The preceding sentences might represent a very simplified description of the last steps of the doctoral research process. However, let us look at it from God's perspective. You have worked with God throughout the research process, from the beginning until now. As you enter the room for your final defense, it may seem as scary as it was for the High Priest to enter the Holiest Place, into the actual revealed presence of God. But you don't enter alone. You *really* don't enter there alone. As the High Priest was enveloped with a cloud of burning incense when he entered the Holiest Place, you are enveloped and almost hidden in the cloud of the Holy Spirit's presence. Our Lord Jesus made a promise to his disciples:

> I will ask My Father and He will give you another Helper. He will be with you forever. He is the Spirit of Truth. ... The Helper is the Holy Spirit. The Father will send Him in My place. He will teach you everything and help you remember everything I have told you. (John 14:16, 17, 26, NLT)

The Holy Spirit has worked with you, guided you, and protected you throughout your research project. He will not abandon you in that moment. He will wrap you in the sweetness of His presence.

To give you additional assurance as you enter this room, the written scrolls of Scriptures (the book of the law at that time), lying next to the Ark of the Covenant, will be a constant reminder of God's word that is with you (Hag. 2:5). The Holy Spirit will use God's word to reassure you and give you holy thoughts, reminding you of the biblical foundations of your research. He will also put His words in your lips, as Isaiah reminds you (Isa. 59:21).

Furthermore, as you enter this defense room (whether in person or virtually), also remember that, just as the High Priest entered the Holiest Place with the blood of the sin offering, you are entering this place not only as a mere human being, but as someone who has been fully redeemed and covered by the blood of Christ. You are not simply a researcher, but a *Christian* researcher whose identity has been transformed into God's chosen instrument, holy and dearly loved by Him (Col. 3:17) because of Christ's redemptive blood—because of Christ himself who is the propitiation or atonement for our sins (1 John 2:2). You have completed this research because of Christ's calling on your life.

Finally, you enter this defense room while being very conscious of the glory and the majesty of God (of which the cherubim are an image). Your research has revealed to you a new aspect of His glory that He calls you to share with your community through your proposed or your already-initiated transformational action plan. His glory will thus shine in a very special way through your presentation in front of your defense jury. You will glorify God in making public that which he has led you to discover and strategize.

In a summary, the whole Trinity is there with you and you are enjoying God's Triune presence in the Holiest Place! Richard Rohr's (2016) concluding words might be an encouragement to you:

Suddenly, this is a very safe universe.
You have nothing to be afraid of.
God is for you.
God is leaping toward you!
God is on your side, honestly more than you are on your own. (p. 282)

Going Out …

You are in God's presence! You have enjoyed stepping forward in this new, living, life-giving, open way into God's presence and His company, as we have seen in the first chapter of this book. You have performed during months and years this love-dance with our triune God in an appreciative, relational and incarnational quest to co-create with God an innovative approach to solving the problem God has put on your heart and called you to solve. Throughout the process, you have discovered and enjoyed so much more of God's manifold grace, His righteousness, and His life-giving *shalom*. As you have worshipped in God's presence throughout the process and in the final stage of the affirmation of your findings in the company of God (your defense jury), you will be ready to walk out of the sanctuary, radiating with God's glory and joy, to share with the people of God waiting outside the tabernacle the good news of God's seal of approval on your research.

Like the people of Israel who celebrated Yom Kippur, or like Nehemiah who organized a celebration (Neh. 8), you will organize a celebration too! But not in a small circle. Nehemiah called all the people together to communicate God's word to them. Similarly, you will need to go out and share your findings with your research community, expressing yourself in such a way that they may understand the joy with which the Lord has filled you. You will not do that alone. You will call on your research partners, your personal learning community, and explain to your people what God has shown to you and what the steps forward will look like.

May I suggest that, with your team, you seek the Lord's face to understand what the next steps might look like (if you have not done that already as part of your recommendations and action plan)? Here are some questions that you may want to reflect on as a team:

- *What exact changes are you praying for ...*
    - *In yourself and what you control?*
    - *In situations where you have some influence?*
    - *In your research community?*
- *If you had four hours right now to begin working on these changes, how would you spend them?*
- *What else will you do to follow through within one week?*
- *What else will you do within one month?*
- *What else will you do within three months, depending on what happens in the early stages?*
- *(Adapted from Nussbaum, 2007)*

A Blessing

Blessings on you as you look for the practical implications that grow naturally from your findings. May the Holy Spirit grant you inspired ideas and the right combination of passion, wisdom and power as you implement them! (Nussbaum, 2007, p. 139)

What about the Humility Gap?

As we rejoice in the completion of the research project, Nussbaum (2007, p. 143) reminds us that God has provided us with a *humility gap*. Realizing this gap will keep you humble as you develop the outcomes of your research. We might quickly discover that we omitted one unforeseen indicator, or that we missed some information that would be helpful, or that more questions are emerging as the implementation unfolds, or that out-of-control events have caused the implementation to take a different turn. These are constant reminders that God is in control of our finitude and keeps us humble and dependent on Him. Instead of feeling discouraged, let us remember that, on this earth, "nothing in all creation will ever be able to separate us from the love of God that is revealed in Christ Jesus our Lord" (Rom. 8:39). And we can count on God who is "able, through his mighty power at work within us, to accomplish infinitely more than we might ask or think" (Eph. 3:20).

Furthermore, although it has been driven by you as a researcher, this final offering or dissertation research is the product of a major team effort. You have worked in collaboration with your personal learning community, your professors and mentors, your field communities, and others. You have depended heavily on each team member—perhaps more than you have ever realized. What about reflecting on ways to thank them for their support?

Take time to thank the Lord and pray for each of the community and team members who have faithfully supported you. Like Paul in Romans 16, make a list of all your helpers, pray for each one, and discern how you can personally thank them!

Realizing that the final offering is actually the product of collaboration by a huge team will keep you humble and thankful. Realizing that you still have a lot of work to do in order to implement your action plan and develop your calling as a servant to your community will also help you remain humble and dependent on the guidance of the Holy Spirit, and on the team members who will work with you!

Peter's recommendation is still pertinent for each of us, especially if we are in leadership positions or will move into them as an outcome of our successfully completed research: "Humble yourselves, therefore, under God's mighty hand, that he may lift you up in due time. Cast all your anxiety on him because he cares for you" (1 Pet. 5:6–7, NIV). God will do the lifting up!

What's Next?

Together, throughout this book, we have experienced how to enter into God's most intimate presence in the company of our High Priest, our Lord Jesus Christ. We have gone through the various steps of moving forward in our research with Him. We have seen Him in so many metaphors drawn from the tabernacle in the desert. We have seen the multifaceted grace of God in so many ways, both through the tabernacle imagery and through our Lord's detailed and practical interventions and guidance in your dissertation journey.

Chapter 7: In God's Presence

I would like to leave you with this blessing that was given to me before one of my challenging trips to Congo many years ago, and that I have treasured in many ways since:

> Now may the God of peace, who through the blood of the eternal covenant brought back from the dead our Lord Jesus, that great Shepherd of the sheep, equip you with everything good for doing his will, and may he work in us what is pleasing to him, through Jesus Christ, to whom be glory for ever and ever. Amen. (Heb. 13:20–21)

References

Ang, F. P. S. (2021). *Developing a transformational leadership model for Malaysia marketplace ministry for human flourishing and cultural impact.* Ph.D. dissertation, Bakke Graduate University. https://bgu.edu/dissertations/developing-a-transformational-leadership-model-for-malaysia-marketplace-ministry-for-human-flourishing-and-cultural-impact.

Bakke Graduate University. (2022). Transformational leadership perspectives taught at BGU. https://bgu.edu/programs/transformational-leadership-perspectives.

Chan, D. (2018). A prayer for the work of Christian scholars. https://blog.emergingscholars.org/2018/07/a-prayer-for-the-work-of-christian-scholars/.

Cleary, L. M. (2013). Cross-cultural research with integrity: Collected wisdom from researchers in social settings. Palgrave MacMillan.

Conner, K. J. (1976). The tabernacle of Moses: The riches of redemption's story as revealed in the tabernacle. City Christian Publishing.

Conceição, S.C. and Hill, L. (2019). *Four-dimensional model for doctoral student support.* [Paper presentation]. Adult Education Research Conference, Buffalo, NY. https://newprairiepress.org/cgi/viewcontent.cgi?article=4109&context=aerc

Cooperrider, D. & Whitney, D. (2005). *Appreciative inquiry: A positive revolution in change.* Berrett-Koehler.

Creswell, J. W., & Creswell, J. D. (2018). Research design: Qualitative, quantitative, and mixed methods approaches. Sage.

Geib, T. (2020). *Quantifying reactive metabolite modifications of target proteins by lc-ms.* Ph.D. dissertation, University of Quebec. https://archipel.uqam.ca/16255/1/D3815.pdf.

Harrison, W. H. (2004). Loving the creation, loving the creator: Dorothy L. Sayers's theology of work. *Anglican Theological Review, 86*(2), 239–257.

Hinojosa, J. and Howe, T.-H. (2016). EPortfolio: The Scholarly Capstone for the Practice Doctoral Degree in Occupational Therapy. *The Open Journal of Occupational Therapy* 4(3). https://www.researchgate.net/publication/304744759_EPortfolio_The_Scholarly_Capstone_for_the_Practice_Doctoral_Degree_in_Occupational_Therapy.

Kiene, P. F. (1977). *The tabernacle of God in the wilderness of Sinai*. Zondervan Publishing House.

Knight, J. A., & Markham, I. S. (2022). *The craft of innovative theology: Argument and process*. Wiley Blackwell.

Lilyquist, C. (1979). *Ancient Egyptian mirrors, from the earliest times through the Middle Kingdom*. Münchner Ägyptologische Studien 27. https://www.academia.edu/44917427/Ancient_Egyptian_Mirrors_from_the_Earliest_Times_through_the_Middle_Kingdom.

Lianputtong, P. (2022). Handbook of qualitative cross-cultural research methods: A social science perspective. Edward Elgar Publishing.

Lygunda Li-M, F. (2018). *Transforming missiology*. Langham.

Marshal, S.M., Klocko, B. and Davidson J. (2017). Dissertation completion: No longer higher education's invisible problem. *Journal of Educational Research and practice*. 7(1), 74-90. https://scholarworks.waldenu.edu/cgi/viewcontent.cgi?article=1231&context=jerap.

Moule, H. C. G. (1841–1920). In Smith, R. (2022). *The scholar's prayer*. https://suchamindasthis.com/2022/07/04/the-scholars-prayer/.

Nussbaum, S. (2007). Breakthrough! Steps to research and resolve the mysteries in your ministry. GMI Research Services.

Oatman, J. (1897). Count your blessings. https://hymnary.org/text/when_upon_lifes_billows_you_are_tempest.

Piaget, J., & Inhalder, B. (1972). *The psychology of the child*. Basic Books.

Richardson, J.E. (2011). *Religious metaphor and cross-cultural communication: Transforming national and international identities*. https://byustudies.byu.edu/article/religious-metaphor-and-cross-cultural-communication-transforming-national-and-international-identities/

Robson, C., & McKarten, K. (2016). Real world research: A resource for users in social research methods in applied settings. John Wiley and Sons.

Rohr, R. (2016). The divine dance: The Trinity and your transformation. Whitaker House.

Saunders, N.K. & al. (2019). Research Onion. Cited in Seuring, S., Stella, T., & Stella, M. (2021). Developing and publishing strong empirical research in sustainability management – Addressing the intersection of theory, method, and empirical field, p. 208. Frontiers in Sustainability. https://www.frontiersin.org/articles/10.3389/frsus.2020.617870/full.

References

Saunders, N.K., Lewis P. & Thornhill A. (2019). *Research methods for business students.* Pearson.

Sverdlik, A. et al. (2018). The PhD experience: A review of the factors influencing doctoral students' completion, achievement, and well-being. *International Journal of Doctoral Studies. 13,* 361-388. http://ijds.org/Volume13/IJDSv13p361-388Sverdlik4134.pdf.

Thom, M. (2017). *The difficulty of practicing fine artists in making a living: Why arts entrepreneurship education is important.* Ph.D. dissertation, London South Bank University. https://www.researchgate.net/publication/319007222_Doctoral_Thesis_THE_DIFFICULTY_OF_PRACTISING_FINE_ARTISTS_IN_MAKING_A_LIVING_WHY_ARTS_ENTREPRENEURSHIP_EDUCATION_IS_IMPORTANT.

Van de Vijver, F. J. R. (2021). *Methods and data analysis for cross-cultural research.* Cambridge University Press.

Vaquera, G.S. (2007). Testing theories of doctoral student persistence at a hispanic institution. *Sociology. 31.* https://core.ac.uk/download/pdf/232537162.pdf

Vincent, L. (2016). A primer on innovation theology: Responding to change in the company of God. Wipf and Stock.

Walland, E. and Shaw, S. (2022). E-portfolios in teaching, learning and assessment: tensions in theory and praxis. *Technology, Pedagogy and Education 31*(3). https://www.tandfonline.com/doi/full/10.1080/1475939X.2022.2074087.

Wormelly, R. (2009). Metaphors & Analogies: Power Tools for Teaching Any Subject. Stenhouse Publishers.

www.ingramcontent.com/pod-product-compliance
Lightning Source LLC
Chambersburg PA
CBHW060420090426
42734CB00011B/2383